A Place for Apology

War, Guilt, and US-Japan Relations

Shu Kishida

Translated by Yukiko Tanaka

Hamilton Books
an imprint of
UNIVERSITY PRESS OF AMERICA,® INC.
Dallas • Lanham • Boulder • New York • Oxford

Copyright © 2004 by
Hamilton Books
4501 Forbes Boulevard
Suite 200
Lanham, Maryland 20706
UPA Acquisitions Department (301) 459-3366

PO Box 317
Oxford
OX2 9RU, UK

Library of Congress Control Number: 2004105491
ISBN 0-7618-2840-4 (paperback : alk. ppr.)

Contents

Preface

Ever since it began with the arrival of Commodore Matthew Perry, who came to Japan in 1853 with his fleet of four warships and forced Japan to open its doors, the relationship between the United States and Japan has been problematic, warped as it were. First of all, the fateful encounter with the rising power after a peaceful slumber of more than two hundred years caused the Japanese psyche to split into two—the outer and humiliated self that worships America (and Europe) and the inner megalomaniac self that disdains the West. For an analogy of this forced relationship, I cannot think of a better one than that of a woman who has yielded to an unwanted sexual advance and opened her body. As I see it, the US-Japanese relationship is not free from trauma even today.

There is a major perception gap, moreover, between the two nations concerning the beginning point of US-Japan interaction. From the Japanese point of view, forced opening was a humiliating event in which the weaker Japan had yielded to powerful America. In the American view, on the other hand, the visit led barbaric Japan out of her silly isolationist policy into more advanced civilization, for which America ought be thanked. With a large gap in perception at the very beginning of their relationship, a major quarrel was perhaps inevitable.

As I realized, however, the split in the Japanese psyche had already existed before Commodore Perry's arrival. Japan had experienced it, way back in its past, in her relationship with China. The "Perry Shock," it turned out, simply resurrected the old memory. Unless the Japanese had lived through this split before, and unless a pattern of countering national crisis either with their "outer self" or their "inner self," depending on the situation, had not already been established, the US-Japanese relationship wouldn't have developed in such a warped state. The pathology afflicting Japan today, in other words, cannot be attributed to the Commodore alone, even if he was truly an arrogant intimidator. Furthermore, a large perception gap concerning the historical opening of Japan has been further complicated by the fact that some Japanese (the "outer self" of the nation) see it according to the American point of view.

At the end of the Russo-Japanese war, in 1905, Japan began showing her "inner self," which was hidden till then, causing a more obvious conflict with America. For Japan, it was the right time to allow her "outer self" to retreat and let a part of the repressed "inner self" reveal itself. Simply to repair wounded national pride, Japan thought. America took it differently. Japan won the war with US support, and yet she began acting arrogantly, thought America, concluding that friendly gestures Japan had shown previously were false, deceptive. Japan was not to be trusted, America decided, and was now motivated to knock Japan down.

I believe America reached this conclusion not necessarily as the result of having observed Japan and her reality objectively, but rather under the influence of a need to rationalize a dark history—that of having murdered Native Americans. Conquering the Japanese, in other words, had been the extension of conquering their own Native Americans. If they succeeded in making the Japanese open themselves to accepting the culture of America and of the world (Americans call their baseball, even, "the World Series"), that would show that having failed in converting Native Americans, and resorting to murder many of them instead, hadn't been a fault. Native Americans had refused a superior white culture to keep their barbaric ways. With this history in their minds, Americans had approached Japan with favor and support, and Japan had responded, it seemed, with friendship and gratitude. But these were only appearances. When American anger flared, it took the form of first limiting, then totally banning, Japanese immigration. Americans were of course totally unaware that they had identified the Japanese with their Native Americans, that their anger toward the Japanese was related to their old trauma.

Japan could see America was angry, but as to the reason, she was without a clue. We did nothing to put America at a disadvantage, nor took any offense, nor were antagonistic, thought Japan. Unaware that America saw it as a deceptive tactic, or the unfaithful behavior of getting rid of a friend no longer needed, Japan thought her shifting from the "outer self" to the "inner self" was justifiable and done for good reasons. Threatened and humiliated before, and now suffering from discrimination, it was we who should be angry, countered Japan. Her anger toward America flared up, and this anger invited more American antagonism. The situation escalated in a vicious circle till bursting in the surprise attack on Pearl Harbor.

If anger is based on some concrete issues or problems, it can be eliminated, usually, when the issue is resolved, or problems are solved. But if it stems from a psychological factor that has been pushed into the unconscious, it does not go away easily; it lasts as long as the trauma that has caused anger remains suppressed.

Problems in the relationship between the two nations, as I see it, remain largely unsolved even today, years after the end of the Pacific War. The relationship is not a healthy one based on elements firmly rooted in reality; it stands on mutual misunderstanding. The American approach to Japan is hard for the Japanese to understand, but the Japanese attitude, with its excessive timidity and meaningless bad-mouthing, is also full of contradictions, and often it is nearly impossible to tell what Japan really wants. The relationship of the two must appear very odd in the eyes of a third party.

Indeed, I cannot find a time since the end of the war when Japan made it clear what she wanted. On no occasion have serious and sustained discussions beeb held and produced concrete policies about what position Japan should take in her relationship with the United States. While the government has been representing the nation's "outer self" of a pro-American position, the Japanese public has expressed its anti-American "inner self" in various ways. Also, it looks as though there is a tacit understanding that, while the government takes care of "the outer self," journalists and the Social Democratic Party, with its opposition to everything, will support Japan's "inner self."

But Japan's anti-Americanism has been, still is, merely a mood. With no concrete strategies on how not to stay dependent on America, its position has remained a mere gesture. Journalists in general, for one, tend to express Japan's "inner self" component too readily and irresponsibly. Anti-Americanism shown in Japanese newspapers' editorials is just an idea that makes the writers feel good about themselves. An outlet for the general public, these words have little impact, and that is why the Liberal Democratic Party has won elections over and over again. Their own criticisms of their government exert little influence on US policies.

Considering these circumstances, it is unrealistic to expect Japan to come up with firm and consistent approaches in her relationship with the United States. Both pro- and anti-American factions have only displayed a certain behavior that can be construed as warranting America's scorn and mistrust. Japan ought to find the best possible ways to promote its interests while keeping close ties with the United States, but it hasn't done so. Instead, people have been dispersing their energies in wasteful expressions of a mood.

The American approach to Japan has not been straightforward, either. Because of their "Indian complex," Americans create their own image of Japan, not seeing Japan as she really is. Interpreting Japan's reactions through their own delusions, America has cast mistrust, even hatred, on Japan, in its discrimination against the Japanese. Much of America's antagonism toward Japan was unnecessary and without good reasons. With this in mind, I have to ask what America has gained in her national interest by having a war with Japan, by having killed more than a few million people, and beaten the nation into pulp.

Risking sounding impertinent, I would say that America's "Indian complex" has an adverse effect upon her relationship not only with Japan but with other nations as well. I believe that America is among the most disliked nations of the world (the Korean's hatred of Japan is also strong), and she loses more of her own people than other nations do to the hand of international terrorists. That is, in my assessment, because a certain type of peculiar behavior causes anger and hatred among people outside the U S. America's high crime rate (more than 10,000 are killed by guns every year, compared to fifty in Japan) is also not unrelated. Banning handguns should be effective in curbing homicides, but Americans choose not to do it. Rationalization used to explain the mass-murder of Native Americans, I believe, prevents them from opting for such a choice. Since the country was built upon the power of guns, banning of them without analyzing and overcoming certain aspects of US history would result in the collapse of a *reason d'être*. Thus, they cannot move to banning guns psychologically.

Particularly since the tragedy of September 11, I cannot help but wonder if America has put itself in the dilemma of the vicious circle. In order to maintain an illusion that it is just, America has denied, or justified, all wrong doings, starting with Native Americans and African slaves. Guilt stemming from such denial has been repressed and is projected upon "the other," which exists externally, or, is internalized; it has caused some kind of persecution complex.

A persecution complex would intensify the fear that America would be attacked, for example, by international terrorist groups. When the fear became real (on September 11), it made America resolve ever more strongly that self-defense by way of building a strong military power is the only way to ensure security. (Being unable to give up the individual right to bear arms is directly related to a psychology expressed in the national defense build-up.) Confronting any danger, real or imagined, America responds with attack. But such attack causes anger (either expressed or suppressed) toward America, bringing more persecution complex. Intensified guilt would be suppressed, or projected upon the victims, bringing more of the sense of persecution. America in this state feels that it cannot let any antagonistic forces exist outside of it, or inside, for that matter. It therefore resorts to even stronger military power.

Let's examine the cases of the surprise attacks on Pearl Harbor in 1941 and the bombing of the World Trade Center in 2001. Any attacks without warning, as existed in both cases, are of course inexcusable and cruel, and it is quite understandable for the attacked to be angry and want to strike back. Once an initial shock passes, however, people, though still angry, should start reflecting upon themselves; they should wonder if they have contributed to such an attack. And if they come upon any problems that might have possibly caused such an attack, they should try, so that future attacks could be prevented, to eliminate these problems as much as possible. This task could be done while striking back at enemies, and without forgiving them.

Looking at it from outside, America as a nation seems uninterested in reflecting upon itself in the aftermath of outside attacks. Instead, it concentrates on punishing the attacker, deeming it "evil." It, in other words, immediately assumes the role of being "the just." Furthermore, it seems to believe that the punishment is justifiable no matter how harsh it is.

This American tendency stems, as I discuss in this book, from the way the country treated its Native Americans. American lack of interest in self-reflection is also related to psychic prohibition that stems from the same root. If America were to succeed in overcoming its Indian complex, its relationship with Japan and other nations of the world would improve. The risk of becoming a terrorists' target would also decrease, and so would the nation's crime rate.

Translator's Note

Having grown up in Japan during the post-war occupation years, I am of the generation who received the injection of an unspoken message: the Japanese, who had caused the Pacific War, were bad people. Early in 2001, while in Tokyo, I became acquainted with the work of Shu Kishida, a renowned scholar and social critic. His words, "What has America gained in her national interest by having a war with Japan?" resounded in me when I put down his book, *Nihon ga Amerika wo yurusu hi (The Day When Japan Forgives the United States of America)*. By explaining why a masochistic view about my own country emerged among the Japanese, and how various perception gaps formed in the historical relationship between the Unites States and Japan, the book helped me to better understand the dynamics of the collective psyches of the two lands I call home.

Then, six months later, on September 11, 2001, the now-familiar tragedy in New York and elsewhere occurred. Suicide bombers with roots overseas were able to gain access to American airlines to attack the US homeland. While grasping the strong emotional reactions of the American people to the devastation of that fatal day, which I witnessed on the television screen and heard on the radio, I couldn't help wondering about the near-total absence in their reactions of serious inquiry into "Why?" Even when the initial shock had long subsided, instead of self-reflection much of what I heard consisted of loud voices of revenge, of moral outcry, and a clear resolve to protect the "American way of life." I thought of Shu Kishida's book and felt it had an answer. I decided to translate it into English. Before too long, the US went to war with Iraq, and, interestingly, Kishida had forewarned of this later development in the book he wrote at the end of 2000.

The American national psyche cannot but repeat the same pattern of aggressive invasion in dealing with "the other." This perpetuation will not cease so long as rationalization (why military action is necessary) and illusion (a self-image that America is the "just" nation, for one) continue to dominate the public mind. Gloomy and frightening though Kishida's diagnosis is, there is a prescription for remedy, and if Kishida is correct in diagnosing Japanese trauma and its symptoms, he might be right about "America's illness" as well.

Kishida applies in this book an idea he has developed, based on psychoanalytic theory, of which he is an expert, for interpreting histories and the mechanism of something we might call national mental health. The reader might read the Appendix first, as there Kishida explains this theory with which he analyzes the Japanese and American psyches.

Having lived in the two countries for an equal number of years, I am inclined to say that the US-Japan relationship has some features that it is worthwhile for the American public to contemplate at this point in history; such contemplation might help people better understand other non-white nations.

Many Westerners have written books interpreting Japan and its people, and the Japanese have done the same for American society and its people. We, however, have little opportunity to read and hear about their views on America from the Japanese directly. Near-total lack of translation of the works by Japanese authors into English, although the other way around is hardly the case, is the reason. It is high time to introduce the opinions of a contemporary Japanese scholar and commentator.

I have changed, with author's permission, the title of the book I translated here. The original title does not seem to convey the content fully and accurately. Also, the English version have some lines that are not in the original book, and they are Kishida's reflection on American actions and responses in the post-September 11 era.

The forms of all Japanese names given in the text follow Japanese practice, that is, last (family) name first, then given name.

Yukiko Tanaka
Seattle, August, 2003

Chapter One

Modern Japan as America's Henchman

When Commodore Matthew Perry anchored four steamships off the coast near Edo, now Tokyo, in 1853 with a letter from the president of the United States and insisted Japan open its door to trade, some Japanese, mainly from remote domains but also individual samurais sympathetic to the emperor, strongly resisted this idea. Their position, expressed in a slogan "revere the emperor and expel the barbarians," was an anti-Americanism in today's term. The leaders of the shogunate, which was in a state of decay after two hundrend and fifty years of reign, however, felt there was no choice but to yield the American (as well as the British and the French, who made a similar demand). They had heard about China's devastating defeat in the Opium Wars a decade earlier and Perry was quite insistent in his demands. More immediately, the shogun's councils, aware of America's greatly superior military power, could not risk Edo under the gunfire of the US. Navy. Four years after Perry's arrival, the shogun's government signed a treaty with the United States (followed by Britain, Holland, Ruccia and France), allowing it a jurisdiction onto Japanese soil and limiting Japan's right to tax imports. As all Japanese recognized, it was an unequal treaty, and by signing it, Japan became a tributary, as it were; it was a situation not much different from being colonized.

Many Japanese seem to consider the fact that only Japan, among all Asian countries except for Thailand, avoided the fate of colonization as a sign of their superiority. I believe this sentiment is the result of their self-deception. An independent nation, you see, has to have the right to govern its subjects autonomously as well as fix tariffs and try its subjects in its own courts of law. The treaty the shogun's government signed, however, agreed not to exercise some of these essential rights. By such a treaty, therefore, Japan gave up its claim to be an independent nation.

FROM VICTIM TO AGGRESSOR

It may be true that the shogun's government had no choice, but signing the treaty cost the shogun dearly. With their pride wounded, people stopped supporting the regime, which eventually led to its collapse. The new Meiji government, formed by those who had originally held the position of restoring the emperor and expelling the barbarians, decided in the end to follow the shogun's policy of opening the country. Quite a few years later, in 1900, the Boxers' Rebellion took place, confirming that the Meiji government's decision was right.

The Western powers had been invading Asia to colonize (although they rationalized these invasions by calling their colonies "the burden of the West") They were aggressors, the thugs, willing to use force to control and exploit, and now, they aimed at the giant prey, China. The Boxers' Rebellion was a revolt of the Chinese people against the Western Powers. As an effort to expel foreign invasion, it was similar to what Japan had gone through in pre-Meiji years. As the victim of the Western colonialization policies Japan should have wanted, psychologically and morally, to side with the Chinese, but instead it sent to China 20,000 soldiers, the highest in number, perhaps because of physical proximity, of all the nations involved, and it was primarily Japanese troops that settled the revolt in the end. I've heard that on this occasion the Japanese soldiers took the orders of their commanders well and fought bravely. Japan, in other words, performed her job as a "henchman" to the West very well, and she gained a favorable opinion among the British and American governments. She proved her usefulness as an ally.

Some Japanese argued then for the other option—to resist Western interference and form an alliance with other Asian nations under colonization. The Meiji government leaders thought neither China nor Korea was a strong and reliable ally, however, and rejected such an option. By contributing to the suppression of the Boxers' Rebellion, Japan separated herself from the rest of Asia and joined a band of thugs and exploiters for the reward of trust and the good opinion of her masters. This is the meaning of *Datsua Nyuou* (Leaving Asia, Joining the West), a slogan that was very popular then. It meant that Japan has chosen to side with the assailants rather than seeing herself as one of the victims.

Observing conflicts among the various exploiting nations, Japan then formed a treaty with Britain. Being in the middle of the Boer War in South Africa, it must have seen Japanese military power useful to fend off Russia, which not only stayed on in Manchuria after the settlement of the Boxers' Rebellion but also was intent upon moving further south. Japan had her own fear that Russia might extend its power into Korea. More importantly Japan wanted to enter into a treaty with the world's most powerful nation. Thus, Japan made Russia an enemy and eventually would go to war in 1904, having Britain and its ally, the United States, as her shield.

Japan won the Russo-Japanese War by a small margin. She actually won it thanks to the support of Britain and the United States. Russia then, ravaged by its own revolutionary armies, was on the brink of losing the central control, and the spirit of the soldiers was also at its lowest ebb. Otherwise, Japan wouldn't have won the war. In addition to this stroke of luck, Britain and the United States were quite generous in helping Japan financially as shown in the fact that more than half of the 2,000 million yen spent to fight the war was raised by bonds sold in London and New York. Also, while battleships of the Russian navy were all Russian-made, most of those belonging to Japan, including the *Mikasa*, were built in Britain, others in Holland. Japan clearly didn't won the war on its own.

Many Japanese even today seem to think that Japan started the war with Russia for reasons of her own and won on her own, but clearly Britain was behind the war, encouraging and supporting Japan to fight. In other words Japan was used. As the builder of a large empire, you see, Britain was very good in using other people to fight for her own benefit. Just as she used Nepalese Gruka soldiers to crash the Sepoi Revolt in India (1857–59), she tried to induce Japan to go to war with Russia. Japan indeed responded to that inducement. Britain, I am sure, had envisioned it that way from the beginning. So had the United States.

In March, 1905, Japan captured Feng tien (now Sheng yang) after great difficulty. By then the Japanese army had been close to the end of its capability with both manpower and munitions. Then, with a stroke of luck, Japan had a major naval victory in the Sea of Japan (May, 1905), and at this opportune moment, and at Japan's request, the United States intervened to end the war. As it would have given Russia the upper hand, Japan couldn't have initiated the negotiation to terminate the war on its own. The United States had earlier helped Japan negotiate the ending of the Sino-Japanese war in the Shimonoseki Peace Accord, and this time, peace was made at Portsmouth, Massachusetts.

Now, the question to ask is this: did the United States intervene on these two occasions as a gesture of friendship, considering Japan to be an independent nation in need of assistance? I don't think that was the case. The United States' intervention was more in the nature of a boss taking care of his henchman. But, unlike the Shimonoseki Treaty, the Portsmouth Treaty did not bring Japan any monetary compensation (Japan received only the southern half of Sakhalin Island), and the Japanese public was irate with this result. Violent uprisings took place in various regions of the country, showing dissatisfaction and opposing the Treaty.

I don't know exactly when the Japanese government began lying to its people, but during the war with Russia, it demonstrated a propensity to do so. The leaders of the Meiji government, not trusting the people, must have reasoned that the public was best led into a web of deception for its own benefit. This propensity to lying would stay, and it is primarily through various lies that the leaders led the country into the fatal direction Japan would take. History since then has proven that the government was more stupid than the public it had accused of stupidity. In any event, the government lied about the war with Russia, enthusiastically reporting victories and hiding the fact that the nation was exhausting its capability to continue the war. (No wonder the public wanted to go on fighting, and not surprising also was the irate reaction at the Portsmouth Treaty by the people, who had endured the war.) Pushing facts aside, stories were created and propagated about Russo-Japanese War. They said that Japan won because its soldiers were brave and unafraid of death, because they fought with a spirit that would conquer any difficulties, and because its soldiers were willing to sacrifice themselves for the benefit of other people and because heaven allowed and gods were willing.

The reality was quite different. I've been told that the Japanese soldiers were not so brave nor so self-sacrificing, and the number who became prisoners of war was not insignificant. These, I suspect, are a more accurate picture since most of the soldiers were farmers—young recruits and largely untrained. I also suspect that one of the reasons for the Japanese Army to later begin giving ludicrous moral lessons such as "not to allow oneself the shame of being taken as a prisoner" was because soldiers were so readily taken during the Russo-Japananese war. Alarmed at this fact, the Army leaders overreacted, it seems, directing themselves in the opposite direction, fabricating stories. In any event, the myth of "Japanese soldiers unafraid of death" was derived from the concealment of the real reasons for Japan's victory over Russia.

Now, there may be some among us who are not afraid of death, but I can assure you they are not many. The fact a myth had to be created from a premise based on an example so widely removed from reality—delusions of grandeur, if you will—only points out how desperate a situation Japanese leaders found their nation to be in.

Ever since the reign of the last shogun, Japan had been placed in a situation somewhat similar to a woman who has been raped. Not only had this woman accepted her rapist, she had decided to follow him. Humiliation, a sense of defeat, and an inferiority complex were natural consequences of such a decision. In order to escape these negative feelings, a myth had to be created. In other words, people had to believe that Japan had won the war with Russia not because of foreign support but because their own soldiers had special qualities and because the Japanese people were capable and willing to do whatever they had to. I believe it was this myth about the soldiers not afraid of dying that led Japan astray and into the war that ended with devastating defeat in the Pacific. The price you pay for denying unpleasant realities and falling for a myth that suits one's needs is unimaginably high, indeed.

GERMINATING HOSTILITIES

Under the assumption that Japan was grateful for being able to leave a backward, barbarous state to join civilized nations under her guidance, the United States was friendly and bestowed favor to Japan until Russo-Japanese war ended with Japan's victory. She was willing to continue looking after her little brother as Japan was also useful as an outpost in Asia. She had no idea that Japan had been wounded, that she was suffering from something like the aftermath of a rape.

It is an American characteristic, I think, not to be very sensitive toward a nation whose pride it has damaged. It is their blind spot. They wouldn't comprehend an old Japanese saying, "Even an inch worm has soul of half-an-inch." I believe there is a historical basis for this insensitivity. The United States, you might say, is a country built and expanded by killing and taking away the pride of the native inhabitants of the land. In order to survive such a history, callousness is a necessity. Because of her blindness and insensitivity, however, America has caused unnecessary conflicts all over the world. These I believe were also a factor in Japan's starting war with her, but America probably hadn't dreamt that Japan would fight so fiercely and desperately for so long.

As an example of this American characteristic, you might recall the historical conference that took place twenty-some years after the end of the Vietnam War, in which the American delegation, including Robert MacNamara, Secretary of Defense during the war, met with then high ranking Vietnamese military leaders. Reflecting upon the war, MacNamara reportedly said then that he had thought Vietnam would readily surrender, recognizing their casualties wouldn't be small. But they didn't do so, he said, because the Vietnamese leaders didn't think highly of the lives of their people. This insensitive remark, of course, angered the Vietnamese delegates. MacNamara, who is reputed to be a "human computer" capable of accurate and speedy cost analysis, you see, couldn't consider the possibility of the Vietnamese choosing to fight at a great human expense. Three million Vietnamese (roughly the number Japan lost in its Greater East Asia War) died in order to save their pride as it were.

Failure to reflect upon other people's pride as a major factor in interpersonal dynamics is a trait seen among many Americans. On the matter of national pride, America, the super-power with its military as well as economic strength, turns its blind eyes to other nations in more recent years.

The Japanese, of course, have their own blind spot. It is my theory that modern Japan, especially in her relationship with the United States, has been split into two opposing forces: self-deprecating worship of the West, which makes up what I call "the outer-self" and "the inner-self," which is furnished with grandiose ideas and animosity toward the West. Until it won victory over Russia, Japan had hidden its inner-self, presenting its outer-self to the outside world; it had acted with humility, behaving as one aware of its subordinate status.

Flush with victory over Russia, however,Japan began revealing its inner-self. Having failed to properly assess the reasons for her victory, she let herself drown in her deluded national pride. This revelation infuriated America, the boss. "Who do you think helped, you insolent?" the boss must have thought, "Don't you dare think you've won the war on your own and don't act as if you were your own boss." So, as early as in 1907, two years after the Russo-Japanese war ended, the US Congress passed legislation, limiting Japanese immigration. Japan was taken by surprise at this development.

As a backdrop to the conflict developing between the US and Japan was also the fact that the two countries were face to face in the Pacific: one, having won the war with Spain, just added Guam and Philippines to its territories, and the other, having won the wars with China and Russia, as well as being on the winning side in the First World War, secured a footing in Korea, Taiwan, Manchuria and the South Seas.

I wonder if anyone recalls the offer made by the United States in 1909, to join in the venture of constructing the Southern Manchurian Railway. Japan turned down the offer, and that didn't sit well with the Americans. Considering the size of the economic and military demands of the project, as well as potential enhancement of international prestige, perhaps Japan should have accepted the offer. If so, in hindsight, she wouldn't have had to go through such a difficult time in raising the necessary funds to increase military spending to fend off Russia and its successor, the Soviet Union. Even the war with America might have been avoided. Euphoric by her victory in the Russo-Japanese war, however, the Japanese felt they were entitled to all rights in Manchuria. Not having shed an once of blood while Japan had lost 200,000 lives (relatively small compared to the 3.1 millions lost in Greater East-Asia War, but ten times more than Sino-Japanese War casualties), America had no right to go into Manchuria, they must have felt. The price Japan paid in the war with Russia was so huge that accepting a joint venture offer from a party who didn't lose a single life, I reckon, was not easy; the offer might have rendered an unacceptable attitude—one haughty, shameless and abrasive.

The Japanese refusal was hard to swallow from the American point of view. Japan was supposed to be their subordinate. America might have considered, furthermore that for a nation of non-white people to have an ambition to build its own colonies was nothing but insolent. The Japanese should know where they stood, it concluded, and in 1924, the US Congress passed an immigration law, which was worse than that of 1907 in singling out the Japanese among all Asians upon whom to close the door. The United States also began large-scale naval training operations on the sea off Japan. Demonstrating their intention in such a fashion would be repeated later in the seas off Taiwan and the Arabian Gulf. It's an American habit but Japan felt harassed by these actions.

I believe Japan, too, did a few things that can be considered irritating. There is a difference in the manner in which the two nations conducted themselves however. While America acted with a clear intention and purpose, Japan aggravated the US unknowingly. Well aware of the US military's superior power, Japanese leaders wouldn't dare to do anything that they knew would trigger American anger. Japan, for example, held a party for the crews when US naval operations were held, pretending not to see the true intention behind the operations. Such a gesture did nothing, of course, to improve Japan's relationship with the United States.

Whenever antagonism sets in, it usually escalates. So, the US-Japanese relationship worsened, and it is hard to say who was more responsible. Both were to blame, we might say, but since it was the United State who had threatened in the beginning by sending Commodore Perry, while the Japanese had kept themselves in quiet isolation, it is clear who was more aggressive. On the other hand, Japan should have known better, one might say. Not having power comparable to that of the United States, Japanese leaders should have been more diplomatic, more careful; they shouldn't have antagonized America. But then, there was the issue of pride, you see. So it wasn't easy.

MEANING OF THE ATTACK ON PEARL HARBOR

Not doing what it should, Japan instead lost self-control, and the result was the surprise attack on Pearl Harbor. The attack was successful militarily but politically, it was a disaster. I can understand, though, the psychology behind that reckless venture.

The Hull Note (taken by the Japanese military leaders as an ultimatum presented by Cordell Hull of the State Department during the peace negotiations in 1941) was insulting to the Japanese no matter how you read it. The United States teased Japan, I think, by giving conditions no one can swallow. Even Monaco and Luxembourg would have rejected the Hull Note, choosing to go to war, Judge Pearl of India, a member of Tokyo War Tribunal, is said to have remarked. What Japan should've done was to take a stance similar to that taken by the United States—to remain ambiguous and act as if giving serious considerations but not agreeing or disagreeing to anything off hand. Japan, in other words, should've teased back. I am not saying that such a tactic would have worked, but Japanese leaders were not in such a frame of mind then. They were military men, not diplomats after all; straightforward and "pure" in heart, they took everything at face value and let anger take over. In any event, the attack on Pearl Harbor was in a sense a response to the unreasonable challenge made by the United States. One cannot deny at the same time that there was a desire among some Japanese to attempt something like the attack.

My theory about the Pearl Harbor attack is that it had something to do with the ultimatum given to the Japanese many years back by Commodore Perry. It was something like revenge. Having come to Uraga with four war vessels, threatening to use the guns to destroy the capitol, Commodore Perry is said to have handed out two white flags and instructed the Japanese envoy to use them since the shogun's military was obviously not his enemy (Kenichi Matsumoto, *Shirahata Densetsu, The Legend of White Flags*). Conscious or not, the humiliation felt at that time has remained in the mind of the Japanese, and eighty-eight years later, it erupted in the form of the surprise attack on Pearl Harbor. I believe that's what happened. The Japanese naval air operations sank four war ships (more ships were damaged but the major result was to sink four battle ships), you see, and although they could have gone further in their attacks, they stopped there. Why? Although the reason for this in not clear (therefore, the commander of this operation were later criticized for not having gone further), to me it is not incomprehensible. After having destroyed four ships—since Commodore Perry brought four warships—the Japanese naval commanders felt satisfied: the revenge was done. A joke, of course, but only partially.

One might go so far as to say that Japan's war with the United States concealed an element of revenge against Commodore Perry. This perception I hold as a Japanese, is shared, I suspect, by Americans as well. When, for example, Japan's surrender was signed on the Battleship *Missouri*, anchored in Tokyo Bay, on September 2, 1945, General MacArther arranged for the flags Commodore Perry's ship had carried to be hung. The implication was obvious. "You might have wanted to revenge the old Commodore but such was a wild dream, and you better understand that you are now to do exactly what you have been told then," those three flags meant to say.

For President Franklin D. Roosevelt, who had wanted his country to go war to aid Britain precariously defending herself against Nazi Germany, Japan's attack on Pearl Harbor meant a golden opportunity. He had needed Japan to take the first step in starting the war, you see. He might also have been looking for an opportunity to totally knock Japan down. Since the United States is a democratic nation, the president needs enough support of the public, not to mention the Congress, in order to start a war. Making the other party a bad guy is necessary to stir up hatred among the public and charge them to go to war, a tactic America has used elsewhere. In the war with Mexico in 1846–48, for example, it was the Mexicans who first invaded US territory. In the Vietnam War, America used the incident in the Gulf of Tonkin (later exposed as a lie made up by the US military) as a rational for the bombing of North Vietnam. Made up or not, America needs the other party to take the first step in starting a war. In this sense, the surprise attack on Pearl Harbor was exactly what Roosevelt had wanted and by giving him the badly needed rational, Japan in effect handed her adversary an advantage.

But still, I cannot say I fully understand why Roosevelt wanted to go to war with Japan. There must have been military and financial reasons, as well as a political one, but in my mind his personal negative feeling toward the Japanese was a crucial factor. Not clear exactly why but he held feelings that might have been inspired by the history held between the two countries. He, as an American, must have experienced a strong reaction to Japan's having moved beyond the original status as America's henchman—the position held in the American perception of Japan following the 1858 Treaty.

American antagonism toward Japan, you see, didn't stem from the fact that Japan had actually wronged America; it was a subjective feeling. Since it was the US who had brought Japan out of a backward state to see the light of modernity, Japan should be thankful, the American sentiment maintained; she should be happy to remain America's grateful little brother. When Japan began asserting herself, even becoming arrogant, and acted as a nation capable of standing on her own, many Americans didn't like it. Although the damages and human losses were real, the attack on Pearl Harbor was something like being bitten by one's own dog to those people. But the Japanese, for whom attacking the enemy's military base was to gain an advantage, failed to grasp the ferocity shown in American anger. From American point of view, the anger was justifiable, like a good person being betrayed by someone who owes him a great deal. It is our human tendency to react with particularly strong anger when a person, to whom we have given a special favor and guidance, betrays, and when that happens, we tend to go after the betrayer with a vengeance, trying to reduce him to his prior state. If the cruelty mustered up to drop atomic bombs is seen in this light, you see, one can understand many things. Those bombs were intended to put Japan back to its original barbaric state.

I believe, however, there was another more fundamental cause for American anger at Japan and the Japanese. It is in their nation's history of having killed native inhabitants to near annihilation. What I speculate also is that the Japanese were physically and psychologically identified with Native Americans. In the collective American consciousness, conquering the Native American and defeating the Japanese were superimposed. As I see it, the two cases of conquering were directly connected.

We can more fully understand about severe criticism raised toward what is known as the "Death March of Bataan," where many American POWs died, if we look at it in the light of what had happened to the Native American. The United States government had made some Native Americans go under similar death marches, in one of which the Cherokees were said to have lost 4,000 out of 17,000. I will come back to the issue of Native Americans later, but let me say that we tend to become more irate in blaming others when we have committed a similar wrongdoing ourselves and managed to get away with it; it is because the guilt is then externalized.

HUMAN ELEMENTS

International relations, in my opinion, are not so different from our interpersonal relationships. Being human endeavors after all, they are neither more complicated, nor harder to understand. You might think that our individual behaviors are controlled by our emotions while dealings between nations are conducted rationally and with cool calculation. I don't believe that is the case. Only those ignorant of group dynamics would say right decisions can be reached by a group of people. The right course of action, I believe, can be found by the three considering the matter very hard independently and without the influences of the other two. In a group situation, as you know, we tend not to think so hard, hence we are unable to achieve wisdom. Groups as a whole tend to behave by far more blindly than capable members of a group acting individually. It is safer, therefore, to assume that when a nation deals with another nation, many follies can be committed. We often see people quarrel and kill each other for no good reason; it is the same with groups.

I don't think America entered into war with Japan after having weighed the pros and cons rationally and reaching the conclusion that it would benefit the country. Having by far more resources, it must have been quite confident in winning the war, but there was nothing beneficial for America except for a sense of satisfaction in defeating. Japan was neither a threat nor in a clear conflict, and yet, it was somehow conceived as a threat. Japan's advance in China had to be stopped, you might say, but in the end the United States helped a Communist regime to be established there, inviting a spread of Soviet influence in East Asia. Its official reason was to beat fascist Japan in the name of freedom and democracy, but this did not make sense either. Not functioning well and far from satisfactory, Japan had a parliamentary system while China was under the dictatorship of Chang Kai-Shek, and the Soviet Union was a communist regime under Stalin.

There were a few Americans, G.F. Kennan among them, who accurately saw what was going on and advised against going into the war that wouldn't bring anything good. Well, Kennan was right. America became involved in the Korean War, which could have been avoided altogether had there been no war with Japan, and 33,000 American soldier's lives would have been spared. The war with Japan also caused America a bad name as a nation that used nuclear weapon for the first time in mankind's history. All of these facts make you wonder what American leaders were thinking. For their own sake, they shouldn't have made a war with Japan, and, of course, the same can be said about the Japanese leaders. The war in the Pacific was an unnecessary war, indeed.

As we know, strategy of the United States in making policies toward Asia has always been to side with either China or Japan. The reason the United States favored China prior to the war while placing Japan in a hostile position was because China was more conciliatory and because Japan had become aggressive. If I repeat what I have said earlier, America's animosity toward Japan stemmed from the fact that it began acting as if it were a big shot; it stopped being a benign little brother. I really can't think of any other good reasons.

We must consider, however, that in the United States the popularity of a president tends to rise when a war starts (we've just seen this in the Iraqi War, for example). This makes me wonder if Americans love presidents who go to war; it also makes me wonder if this was one of the reasons behind Roosevelt's decision. One must not blame only him, however, since the same can be said about Japanese leaders. Wanting to keep its popularity among the public was one reason, among others, why the Japanese military went on fighting in China.

Although I can see why Japanese leaders were upset about the way the United States had been treating Japan, I find it difficult to understand why they couldn't let it go. What exactly were they thinking when they decided to start a war with no chance to win? As we now know the United States had industrial power ten times larger than that of Japan. It was obvious that Japan would lose. I can sympathize, but I must say the Japanese leaders were not very clever. It is easy for me to say all these in hindsight, I realize, but had they not have started the war despite such humiliating circumstances, historians would have counted them, no doubt, among the great leaders of the world. Japanese leaders were unable to see the obvious, but to know facts and to understand the weight of those facts are two different things, I suppose. Seeing Germany's great successes in their surprise attacks, therefore, they might have deluded themselves and thought they had a chance as well.

I question the validity of the rationale of the Japanese military for starting the war not from where we are today but from where they were at that time. America, having won the war with Spain and obtained the Philippines, and being on the way to establish a foothold in China, you see, could not allow Japan to be a counter-power in Asia. It could not allow Japan to join the Western Powers in invading and colonizing Asia, thus the Hull Note.

To accept the conditions of the Hull Note meant for Japan to lose without fighting, since the Note demanded, in short, that Japan withdraw to its original position, to be a henchman serving America. Japan refused the Hull Note and went to war. It lost the war and found itself in the same place America had originally insisted. America, in other words, succeeded in achieving the conditions spelled out in the Hull Note. It was just like a henchman decided to rebel against his boss by refusing to go back where he had been, and when he gave the first punch in defiance, a hundred punches came back, putting him back to his old place. In my assessment, this is the essence of the war between America and Japan.

Accepting or refusing the Hull Notes, it turned out, was the same for Japan. The question to ask, then, is whether or not Japan was better off by going to war. As I have often heard, the choice was between sudden and large poverty by fighting the war and gradual impoverishment by avoiding it. Having decided doing something was better than nothing, Japan went to war, knowing its great disadvantages. Military leaders have rationalized that they couldn't let the people down as Japan's Imperial Army and Navy ought to be the pride of the people who had been sacrificing their personal well-being via stiff taxation. Insistence of no retreat without fighting, however, was nothing but a rationalization. If they don't fight, they would lose their face, they also said to themselves, putting their reputation as their first concern. I suspect they also wanted the world to see, even for a short while, what fine soldiers they had created with such pain and devotion.

American leaders didn't think highly of the Japanese and their military capability. In fact, they thought Zero fighter planes were flown by German pilots. Although they had sought an opportunity to go to war with Japan, they didn't expect it not only succeeding in attacking Pearl Harbor, but to go further by occupying Singapore and Burma in the west, the Aleutian Islands in the north, the Dutch East Indies (Indonesia) in the south, even as far as New

Guinea; they never dreamed that Australia would be bombed. Furthermore, they had no idea that the war would trigger various Asian nations to begin their full-fledged struggles to free themselves from colonization and achieve independence. If this consequence had been foreseen, the United States may not have dragged Japan into the war.

It was also a big mistake to let their colonies be occupied by the Japanese military, to have it show the people, in effect, how to fight against white colonizers. When the war ended, the first order the Allied Forces gave the Japanese Army, it is said, was not to give any weapon to the native populations. Realizing their mistake no doubt, they tried to correct it as quickly as possible.

The greatest loss Japan suffered by fighting and losing the war with America clearly was the lives of 3.1 million people. A similar number died in other parts of Asia, and according to Chinese counting (unsubstantiated), the number could be as high as 20 million altogether. I can't think of any other losses worth mentioning. Losing Taiwan and Manchuria shouldn't count as Japan would have lost them sooner or later anyway. As for the gains, I would like to say that the biggest was the de-colonization of Asian nations, but this would have happened in due time even if Japan hadn't go to war. The war speeded the process up a bit, but when the Japanese claim that the war liberated Asia from colonization, they are only trying to justify themselves. Such a claim implies that other Asian nations were incapable of standing up against Western rule without Japanese help.It is an affront toward their fellow Asians.

The other gain, some people say, was that the Japanese freed themselves from the dictatorial rule of the authoritarian and foolish military leaders, and that democracy and freedom were introduced as the result. In my opinion, this is another rationalization. It is a rational employed by Americans and Americanized Japanese, but also by people in need of shielding themselves against the shock of having lost the war. As is with the argument of freeing colonized Asia, this rationalization is based upon the assumption that the Japanese people were incapable of rescuing themselves from their own warmongering dictators without American help. It is an affront to the Japanese people.

Having fought the war may have shown the world that the Japanese were not a subservient people readily giving in under the threat from a powerful country like the United States; that they were willing to fight back even when huge sacrifices were anticipated. But this gain has been nullified, I have to say, since Japan after the defeat has been existing as a servile nation; that is, as America's henchman.

Considering both gains and losses, do we say Japan shouldn't have gone to war with America? Or, shall we settle for the notion that Japan had no choice? The loss was far greater than the gain, and therefore, I must conclude that Japan made a foolish move.

Chapter One

HISTORY OF HUMILIATION

I would say both the United States and Japan are like organized groups of gangsters—the former was bigger, more powerful and the latter, a small-timer under the wing of a big boss. As I have said, the small-time gangster let himself be deluded when he achieved victory over Russia, thinking he was equal to big guys. What defeated Russia was not the small-timer's own strength but he misunderstood. His boss didn't like this and decided it was time for the small-timer to realize, before he gets more arrogant, who had supported and helped him. To put him in line, as it were. The big guy, America, did many things to irritate and provoke the small-time gangster Japan. So much so that the latter felt he had taken as much beating as he could, but no more. Having summoned enough courage, he defied the boss, and, for the one punch he gave, he got a hundred back in return.

That Japan took it all until finally no more, however, was a Japanese view. American interpretation was that the Japanese were cunning liars. They had been deceptive all along; having pretended to be peace loving, and put their boss off guard, and then, they leaped on.

In the winter of 1941, when Pearl Harbor was attacked, the German troops, you recall, were being pushed back near Moscow, making their defeat more certain. Japanese military leaders had this information but decided to ignore it. Not taking their eyes off earlier quick and successive victories of the German campaigns, they remained dazzled and optimistic; German success was crucially important for them at that point. Because they desperately wanted to believe that no matter how slight the chance was Japan might win, they let themselves be deluded and went on hoping against their good judgment. As we now know, the Japanese military had a bad habit of ignoring facts it did not want to confront. It was this tendency, in my mind, that hastened Japan's defeat.

A strong desire to win the war with America, you see, was firmly rooted in the minds of the military leaders. Ever since the Japanese had faced Commodore Perry's threat with total powerlessness, the Japanese have lived with a sense of humiliation pushed somewhere deep in their mind. One hundred and some years history of modern era in Japan, in fact, was that of continuous humiliation. The nation was determined to free itself from such a state and regain its pride; people were eager and impatient. The delusion that Japan had won the war with Russia on its own stemmed from a need to alleviate this sense of humiliation. And, since it was America who had brought the humiliation in the beginning, Japan had to fight against America, to finally get over it.

Many Japanese were overjoyed at the news of the successful attack on Pearl Harbor. They felt the day of clearing their long time grudges had finally arrived. The six months between this attack and the battle at Midway was the only time when they were happy, enjoying a relief from the sense of humiliation. And, this brief happiness was obtained in exchange for 3.1 million lives. It was a high price no matter how you cut it. After the disastrous defeat in the battle of Midway, however, Japan was on the the losing path, rolling down a steep slope to the bottom, as it were. And, from that point on Japan has been under American control; their subject, if you will.

Japan today accepts the position of a henchman in a matter-of-fact way, paying a due so that she can run her own business. Although problematic incidents such as rapes of Japanese girls in Okinawa by US Marines take place, many Japanese are contented because their country is under US military protection and because they are able to conduct lucrative businesses. These people have suppressed their sense of humiliation by deluding themselves into believing that the United States is Japan's "equal" ally and that they are in "mutual" agreement in the Security Treaty. Most of the time they are successful in this suppression and self-delusion, but once in a while their smothered humiliation asserts itself and erupts. We've seen those eruptions on such occasions as the large-scale anti-Security Treaty uproars of the early 1960s, an attempt on the life of US ambassador Edwin Reischauer, the hijacking of the airplane *Yodo*, ritual disembowlment of Mishima Yukio, and the atrocity committed at Tel Aviv Airport by members of the Japanese Red Army. Most recently, it was seen in the form of terrorism by the cult of Oum Shyinrikyo.

Chapter Two

Two Kinds of Self-Delusion
to Repress A Sense of Humiliation

Japan today is like a person who makes a living conducting various businesses for which he has to pay a fee. The nature of US-Japan relationship today is that of a big boss and his henchman who has to be on guard not to displease his boss.

People in Japan may think the United States and Japan are equal partners and allies, but objectively speaking, that is not the case. Although they wouldn't openly admit it, I think Americans know it. So does the rest of the world. First of all, Japan depends on America for her defense, and it gives the use of vast land to the US military. Japan is keeping the Constitution written and imposed by the United States, and whenever a new Prime Minister is selected, he makes a visit to Washington. As if this were still the time of shoguns, when local lords were obliged to make an annual trip to Edo to show their loyalty.

Assessing these facts in a cool, objective manner, one has to conclude that the two countries are not in an equal relationship. Ever since 1945, you see, Japan has been an occupied country, an America's subject, if you will.

DENIAL OF REALITY

If such is the case, the Japanese should naturally feel humiliated, but they don't seem to be. Their nation's subordinate relationship to the United States is obvious to others but the Japanese themselves don't see it that way. What it is, in my opinion, is that they feel humiliation but are repressing it. To put it another way, they know it in their heart but pretend not to notice. They are deluding themselves. This psychic mechanism of self-delusion is commonly found among the Japanese since the end of the war. Every time they face a problem that needs to be solved, their delusion has gotten in the way, and in the end, the problem is left unsolved. If its wall could be broken, a possibility to solve problems would open up. The Japanese haven't been able to do so, thus the ensuing frustration, dissatisfaction and restlessness, which have been piled up over the years. A sense of instability and of being closed in, sometimes depressive moods as well as general discomfort, are all, in my opinion, due to this self-delusion.

What to do, then? The first step of the task that I propose is to see the situation accurately and recognize that Japan is an occupied nation. Then, if people have enough strength required to leave such a state behind, they should work toward that goal. If they don't have that strength, there's nothing that can be done; they must accept the reality and wait till the time comes.

It is hard, even painful, for the Japanese to admit that their country is a henchman, that it is in a state of occupation. However, this is an old story, to think about it. Although not as bad as it is now, the Japanese have experienced this humiliation earlier when they were forced to open themselves up and enter the power game of the modern world. The country's history ever since has been that of dealing with pain and the doubts that go with it. And, after the defeat in the war with the United States, the Japanese found themselves being cornered even further into the same predicament. Having failed in a major way in the task they had launched during the Meiji era, and now with so many issues still left unresolved, the Japanese are not sure what to do.

If you and I find ourselves in a circumstance that causes a sense of humiliation, it is best, generally speaking, to first recognize such a state and, then correct it, if possible, so that we no longer have to feel humiliated. But at times, we fail in such an attempt. For example, when we are weak and the party we are up against is overwhelmingly strong. Then, we might opt to delude ourselves in order to get rid of the sense (although this is not really getting rid of it). And there are two ways to do so. Since painful states consist of two elements—the reality that causes humiliation and the fact that we are powerless and unable to change such reality—we can presumably set ourselves free, granted only subjectively, by denying either one of them.

The first kind of self-delusion has to do with the latter element mentioned above, that is, while recognizing that the situation is humiliating, we deny the fact that we have no power to overcome it and that there's nothing we can do but bear the consequences. This is a way to avoid the sense of humiliation by overestimating our power, by having a megalomaniac self-image. The other kind is to deny the reality causing the sense and say it is not humiliating; the state we are in is humiliating objectively speaking, but we refuse to see it as such, thus keeping ourselves free from the sense of humiliation. Whether or not we have the power to change the reality isn't an issue here. The first is to deceive ourselves (about our limitations and powerlessness) and the other is to turn a blind eye to the outer world (and the circumstance we are in).

Either way, we are deceiving ourselves so that we solve the problem temporarily. Ever since they relented and accepted an unequal treaty under Commodore Perry's threat—a rape, as I call it—the Japanese have been practicing self-delusion of both kinds: from the beginning of the Meiji period until 1945 they had taken the first approach primarily; from then on, the other.

Now, let us remind ourselves that whether it is with an individual person or a nation, both self-respect and some realistic means for self-preservation are necessary in order to survive. If the first is missing, there's no sense of self-worth, and such a state evokes feelings of emptiness, defeatism as well as the sense of inferiority. Lacking the latter, on the other hand, means that survival itself is in danger; in the worst case death or extinction will result. Normally, we can have both self-respect and means of self-preservation, and we are able to adjust ourselves to the real world outside while maintaining our self-respect internally. At times of crisis, however, this task is not easy, and we feel a choice has to be made. When our lives are threatened by an overwhelmingly strong person, for instance, we will have to chose either to die in order to protect self-respect, or, to give up pride and resort to some measures in order to survive.

The Japanese found themselves in this type of crisis at the end of the shogun's reign. At first, they tried to protect their pride. Those who promoted the position to "expel the barbarians" in fact killed foreign residents (in the 1862 Namamugi Incident, for example) and engaged in battles, attacking foreign ships anchored off Kagoshima (1863) and Shimonoseki (1864). When they were made to realize their grave disadvantages and the recklessness of their attempts, however, they stopped resisting the Western Powers altogether.

The leaders of the new Meiji government were keenly aware that their country was in a humiliating state. Leading it out of such a state was their first political goal, and their immediate task was to abolish the unequal treaties with the Western Powers and to accumulate the national wealth necessary to build military power. The unequal treaties were repealed by the beginning of the twentieth century (in 1911), and by this time Japan was well into becoming a strong military force. Since these two accomplishments were made coincidentally, the leaders confirmed their belief that strengthening the nation's military power was the way to end the humiliating circumstances.

Japan, however, lacked natural resources. With its industries still underdeveloped, the country was also poor, and building a strong military equal to those of the Western Powers was beyond its reach. There was, in other words, a gap between military power needed to erase the sense of humiliation and that which the nation's economic and industrial capability could provide. Military leaders would soon try to fill this gap by forcing their soldiers to make large and numerous sacrifices. It is because of this gap, in other words, that Japanese soldiers would soon undergo atrocious treatment.

As I have mentioned, the Japanese took the victory in the 1905 war with Russia as their own accomplishment, while in reality the war was barely won, and only with a great deal of help from Britain and the United States. This self-deception, in which the Japanese leaders disregarded the facts, was to fill the gap, or, to put it more accurately, to be able to feel it filled.

Lacking the real power necessary to overcome their sense of humiliation and their inferiority complex by way of deliberate measures, Japanese leaders seized a chance to feel superior by ignoring facts that were hard to swallow. They let themselves take flight into a grandiose fantasy. This was how the notion of "brave Japanese soldiers who are unafraid of death" was created. In this myth, Japanese soldiers were without fear and therefore had no enemies, particularly in ground battles. In face-to-face confrontations, they were told, the enemy would retreat as they were coward and fearful of death. (I have a childhood memory of hearing a song girls sang in their play, and it went like this: "The ones who run away are the Russians; those who stay and fight to the death are Japanese, who, facing thousands of enemies, killed all but six.")

Clearly, this notion was created out of propaganda. It was without any realities to back up. Had there been even one case in which Japanese troops won in close combat, for example? Was it in the attack of Lu Shun, or of Feng tien? There were no such cases. High spirit, bravery and other psychological states of soldiers are not all that are needed to win a war, of course (these factors have in fact become less important in more recent wars); funding, weapons, intelligence, and other material support are also of crucial importance. Strategy planning and good supplies are essential as well. In the war with Russia, Japan relied heavily upon Britain and the United States for supplies and funds, but Japanese military leaders wanted to think they had won on their own, so that they were able to rid themselves of their sense of humiliation from years ago. They chose to deny facts and held on to illusion; they ignored physical factors that had contributed to winning the war (which had been supplied by the West) and emphasized psychology (which they had been able to deliver themselves). The same approach is going to be applied to overall strategies of Japan's army and navy in later years.

Thirty-six years after Japan's victory over Russia, the war with the United States broke out The military leaders tried to win this war in the way they had (so they imagined) earlier. As I have said, the victory over Russia had been a fantasy. Now, we know that no war can be won solely on the strength of spirit or psychology, but Japan tried to do so in the war with America, disregarding various elements that existed in reality. People were told that the battle was between the spirit and the material, that their noble spirit would not, could not, be bent by unworthy materialism, and that Japan therefore would win. What supported this deluded notion was a misguided appraisal of the outcome of the Russo-Japanese war. Not having grasped the real reasons for the victory over Russia, but having let themselves fall victim to delusions was the direct cause of Japan's losing the war with the United States. Japan lost the war not because of failures in specific strategies, or because of unfortunate circumstances that piled up, or from some individuals not exerting themselves. It was not even because of an overwhelming shortage of materials.

Japan's defeat was unavoidable. It was obvious even before the war began. Unsuccessful individual campaigns were merely a part of the unrealistic overall strategy conjured up by the military leaders. Operations in Guadalcanal under Commander Tsuji Masanobu and those at Imphal under Lieutenant General Mutaguchi Yasunari were, as we can see now, totally unrealistic, even ridiculous, and they caused many meaningless deaths. While military leaders were responsible for these disasters, putting all the blame on them would take us nowhere, however. In a more normal time, they would be big liars or bluffs to whom no one would pay attention; they would be megalomaniacs without any sense of reality. Because it wasn't that the individual generals and leaders in the Guadalcanal, Imphale and other campaigns happened to be without good sense or ability, we must find elsewhere for an explanation. The real problem, I believe, lies in the fact that the Japanese military was organized in such a way that these individuals were chosen as leaders and given the power to use. An important question to ask, then, is why the Japanese military had such a structure.

"TO BE BRAVE AND UNAFRAID OF DYING"

Japanese military leaders seemed to have convinced themselves that Japan could win the war if their soldiers were brave and not afraid of dying. In my opinion, this ludicrous idea, more than anything else, led Japan to a disastrous circumstance, but military training actually emphasized this idea in order to help soldiers rid themselves fear on the battle field. "To be a warrior is to know one's own death," a line from *Hagakure* (a historical writing on the way of samurai warriors), was referred to with great enthusiasm. Any word about the fear of dying was taboo, and soldiers were sent to the field with such an encouragement as "Go and die honorably!" Where else but in Japan were soldiers sent off with such words? The same idea is also found in many Army songs (a few examples of which are: "Brave is the man who pledges no return without victory" (*The Japanese Army*); "the two of us are true comrades, having exchanged a vow to pick each other's bones/our lives as we know are short"(*Comrades*); "how can we die without a victory/ we who'd been sent off/ with brave words of triumph"(*A Battlefields Song*); and "the night we knew to be our last/ carried the smell of blood crossing the field/ we give our hard glares at the sky taken by the enemy"(*Heroes of the Sky*). As you can see, Japanese soldiers were expected to embrace death, and those who didn't were considered unwilling to fight. To fight meant to die, it seemed. Now something is wrong with this logic, because if you die, you see, you can no longer fight.

To expect any human being not to be afraid of death is unreasonable, and military campaigns based on such an unreasonable expectation will encounter problems soon or later; they are destined to fail. The battle off Leyte Island (the Japanese Navy had a good chance to strike hard at the US force) was lost precisely because the campaign itself was unreasonable; it was a case in which"being brave and unafraid of dying" was held as a blind belief. Because of this unreasonable expectation, a fantasy, really, many unrealistic campaigns were developed and ended disastrously. The reason for this, I let myself repeat one more time, was because military leaders tried, and the public were behind them, to win the war by insisting that their solders were "brave and unafraid of dying." Everyone knows that material supply and intelligence are crucially important to win a war, but the Japanese military did not think so. For example, it did not highly regard men in charge of transporting supplies ("if you can call those in charge of supplies soldiers, butterflies and dragonflies must be birds," a song taunted them). That it targeted warships but neglected to sink supply vessels, that it didn't notice secret codes being broken, and that it didn't think intelligence activities were crucially important, are all related to the notion that the spirit was what's important and other things were negligible. Wretched were the soldiers thrust into warfare with an idea that bravery would overcome fear of death. Any soldiers placed in harsh circumstances with real threats on their lives are all wretched, no doubt, but I believe it is only Japanese soldiers who were forced into an impossible situation of considering the wretchedness an honor bestowed upon them.

In American history, too, we see a similar occasion. When white men's westward advance cornered Native Americans into nearing a total defeat, a superstition, I've heard, was spread, saying that a certain charm would protect them from being shot by the white men, that charm holders wouldn't die even if they were shot. Some Native American warriors believed in this superstition, and they are said to have fought against the US Cavalry with an enormous courage, only to be shot and die. Thinking of the circumstance where these warriors were forced into clinging to such a superstition, one finds it hard to withhold tears, but the myth of Japanese soldiers unafraid of dying was similar to this superstition. However ludicrous, these superstitions were the result of the ruthlessness with which the U S military has cornered those it deemed an enemy.

Japanese soldiers were also given an order not to be captured alive. This was because earlier, in the Russo-Japanese War, they were taken prisoners at an alarming frequency and Army leaders wanted to prevent the same from happening again. But this order meant that soldiers had to fight till they died. From a practical point of view there is no use of going on fighting when weapons and gun supplies are exhausted. When defeat is in sight, choosing to die does no good. Furthermore, dying rather than being captured puts the enemy in an advantageous position because having a large number of prisoners when supplies of food and other necessities are scarce is a problem. If they were to die in large numbers, there would be an issue of responsibility, and executing them would inevitably cause guilt. Indeed, the problem of POWs is a big headache for any nation.

Rather than surrender and be captured, Japanese soldiers opted for death, which was described as "the crash of jewels"; they chose to commit suicide with their banzai charge. From the American point of view, this was quite helpful. As their policy was to try not to keep soldiers in captivity, some American troops are said to have killed Japanese soldiers ready to surrender, rather than taking them as POWs (John Dower, *War Without Mercy: Race and Power in the Pacific War*, 1986), and "crash of jewels" suicides of Japanese soldiers reduced the number of prisoners they had to kill. Being "crashed" as "jewels" is preferable to becoming a prisoner and killed, one might say, but if you become a prisoner, your life may be saved, or there may be a chance for breaking out of the prison and escaping. (I have been told, however, that, unlike American, British and German POWs, Japanese prisoners did not attempt to escape.) Japanese soldiers should not have carried out banzai charges and killed themselves.

When five special submarines (with two-man crews) were sent to participate in the surprise attack on Pearl Harbor, their safe return was not expected. Four sank and the last ran aground, making one of its crew the first Japanese POW, and the nine who died with the special submarines (out of fifty-five who had died in Pearl Harbor attack) were later enshrined as gods. During the war their photos were hung next to those of the Emperor and Empress in many households. This fact points out that the use of these special submarines was for a psychological effect, rather than a part of actual war strategies. It was to urge the entire military, as well as the public, to have resolution similar to that of those ten brave men who went in the submarines.

The *kamikazes* were organized in the fall of 1944 by Ohnishi Takijiro, a Lieutenant-General of the Navy, with a similar intention. A strategy no one had heard of before, it was successful only in the beginning, when there was a surprise effect. Since the American response was quick with such measures as increasing escort fighters and naval artillery barrages, most kamikaze planes ended up crashing into the sea. "One plane sinks one ship" was merely a boast, and while four thousand kamikaze planes were flown, the success rate is said to have been less than five percent. The planes were clearly for a psychological effect—to emphasize how brave Japanese soldiers were. If they had been for a real and practical effect, they would have been discontinued when they proved to be ineffective.

The boast was in vain; it was simply to ease the mind. There was a belief, a hope, somewhere in people's minds, you see, that the situation could possibly reverse itself if extraordinary courage were demonstrated. Some kind of psychological fix was desperately needed at a time when Japan was losing the war. Why did such a reckless campaign not meet opposition, as it most certainly would have in any other country? Perhaps because the Japanese in general, along with the military leaders, believed in the notion on which the campaign was based, that "being brave and unafraid of dying" would somehow bring victory. We call an idea in which we want to believe despite reality pointing to the other way, or which is repeatedly betrayed by reality, a delusion, and the way the Japanese held onto the idea of the kamikaze belongs to the realm of delusion. People deluded themselves because they saw no other way to heal the wounds of the past and recover their pride. What the Japanese had grappled with as they entered the modern world, one must conclude, was an injury very serious in its nature, indeed.

As people would point out later, various campaigns in the war with America lacked a unifying central strategy and were without logic, as well as they were foolishly inadequate. This blame comes from the position that wars are to be fought with well-defined and concrete aims, and from such a standpoint the criticism is to the point. As the kamikaze strategy points out to us, however, the Japanese did not fight the war as a self-defense in any realistic sense, nor for gains for the nation; they didn't go to war to liberate other Asian nations from Western domination, either. They fought in order to protect, or recover, their pride, and they imagined doing so was possible. If we look at the whole situation from this perspective, everything makes sense. Starting with the surprise attack on Pearl Harbor, then to the campaign in August, 1942, in the sea off the Solomon Islands (in which the *Mikawa* sank four US cruisers but missed vital supply vessels), followed by suicidal infantry attacks made on various Pacific islands, the flights by kamikaze pilots, and on to the final failed mission of the battleship *Yamato*: all fit this calamitous theme.

No one can deny that Japanese soldiers fought desperately hard, and their courage was shown in various campaigns. Bravery, of course, is an important factor in order for soldiers to fight well in a war. If soldiers had not been brave, Japan wouldn't have won the Sino-Japanese war; thus the Russo-Japanese war wouldn't have happened, or, even if it did, Japan would have been defeated right away. The Western Powers then would have held Japan in disdain, keeping her under control, much like a colony. The mistake made, however, was giving bravery too much, and delusory, emphasis. Bravery certainly would raise the morale of the soldiers, but the Japanese military leaders made it not a means, but the goal. It was forced upon the soldiers even when it wasn't needed; even when it became a liability—pushing troops into harm's way rather than scoring points over the enemy. The soldier, in other words, had to be brave compulsively. I call it fetishism, using a psychological term. Bravery, in other words, was a fetish object, and strategies built upon fetishism cannot be successful.

Japan's ambitious attempt to eliminate humiliation via the extraordinary bravery of its soldiers failed. Even though the people were united and exerted energy seldom shown before, and probably after as well, the attempt was thwarted because of one major defect. Overestimating its own strength, Japan fell into self-delusion. The attempt failed, in other words, because the idea and the goal were not grounded in reality.

Not only did Japan's self-delusion cause a failure, the failure pushed Japan into a state of more disgrace. It had been merely unequal treaties that made the Japanese feel tied down and not free earlier; the country had not been under foreign military occupation. Defeat in the war with the United States, however, placed her in a more obvious form of control. And so, the government leaders decided they should try the second type of self-deception, denying the existence of humiliation itself. Now the people were to believe that the reality facing Japan did not warrant the sentiment of humiliation.

If we look at the ways the Japanese have dealt with the state of humiliation, we see a clear difference between the means taken by the Meiji leaders and what was done after the defeat in the Pacific War. The leaders of the Meiji government appealed to the world at every opportunity they had, insisting that the treaties Japan had to sign with the United States and other Western nations were unequal and humiliating. They expended a great deal of effort trying to abolish them. The Japan-US Mutual Security Treaty, signed in 1951, on the other hand, has never been defined as unequal; not only has the Japanese government made little attempt to abolish it, but Japan appears to want to keep it forever.

Objectively scrutinizing the situation in which Japan is now placed, however, one would have to say that it is under US control; it is occupied. And yet, not only the government but the people in general are unwilling to view it in that way. They insist that Japan and the United States are equal partners, and that their relationship is based on mutual trust and respect. Having experienced total defeat, they are now firmly resolved not to try to challenge American control in any way. Convinced themselves that the status quo was the only option, they altered their previous perception and concluded there was no humiliation. Nothing is wrong with being under someone else's defensive umbrella, they have decided; such a state is not only acceptable but preferable. These people also want to believe that their country is autonomous, that it makes all decisions on its own without American interference.

BROAD-MINDED AMERICANS

The Japanese accepted US occupation with little resistance because, in my opinion, a shift in focus took place in their self-deception from one type to the other. But there are other factors as well. Their own military leaders' atrocious conduct (although people somewhat exaggerated it during the years immediately after the war) was certainly one of them. Having made mistakes of coming up with poor strategies repeatedly, the military hid the facts of failed campaigns from the public, for example. It did so to save its reputation, I suppose. To protect military secrets, they rationalized, but there was no need to keep the facts of lost campaigns secret, since the enemy already knew about them. In its attempts to hide the fact that the war was being lost, the military also went so far as to transfer soldiers who had fought in various lost campaigns—such as Nomonhaan, Midway and Guadalcanal—to high risk fronts so that other soldiers would not find out about these losses. The public now realized that the callousness with which the Japanese military treated the lives of common soldiers was incomparable. People were made to see that their military leaders were not only wrong in their decision making but pumped up courageous-sounding but empty slogans. The war had been started by these military leaders who demanded the people to "ask for nothing till the victory"; they urged the nation to keep believing in victory despite the number who had lost their families and loved ones, and despite the fact that the survivors had barely enough to exist.

In spite of all these and other extreme hardships, which the people had endured, the war ended in defeat, and with a loss of 3.1 million lives and much of the land scorched and flattened by bombings. The war was meaningless, people concluded, and they were deeply sorry that they had gone along with the military. It is totally understandable that the Japanese were convinced that the war with America (or any war, for that matter) was foolish. No matter what the circumstances had been, they now said, the war shouldn't have happened; Japan now has no choice but to get along with the United States.

The US occupational policy for Japan was quite lenient, and this is another factor contributing to the absence of resistance among the Japanese in the post-war era. Ironically, it was Hitler who had paved the way for this leniency. As we know, in the Versailles Treaty (at the end of World War One), Germany was severely punished by the Allied nations, Britain and France in particular. (If the reparations had actually been paid as indicated in the Treaty, it is said, the total sum would have made it possible for the entire British and French populations to live for several decades without working, while Germans toiled like slaves; Germany lost some of her territory as well.) As World War I was truly horrendous, not only for the soldiers on the front but for civilians as well, one can understand how the Allied Forces were resolved to make Germany pay. This anger was behind such a harsh treaty.

It is not impossible to say that this harshness of the Versailles Treaty contributed World War Two. The Germans were eager to fight again, in part, because they were encouraged to think that only another war could free them from their sense of misery. Hitler, who saw that the British and the French were reluctant to fight again, took advantage of this situation. While Hitler was responsible for the war in which fifty million are said to have been killed, the anger and greed of the British and the French, who went after Germany with such vengeance, was also a factor. This awareness was behind the policies of the US occupational government in Japan, which were perhaps the most broad-minded in the entire history of military occupations.

The Japanese, who had believed till the first day of the occupation that all men would be taken slaves while women were raped, were naturally impressed and felt grateful about the leniency of the US occupation. Although killing and raping by the soldiers of the occupational force did happen in isolated incidents, the difference between them and the behavior of Soviet soldiers on their rampages in Manchuria was like night and day. As I heard, American soldiers' unruly conduct in Japan was rarer than that in Chinese cities occupied by their Japanese counterparts. This relatively problem-free state, I believe, was the result of General Mac Arthur's resolve to make American occupation a success. He is said to have given strict orders that his soldiers were to be kept at bay. (By comparison, American soldiers in Japan today are let lose, it seems. The crime rate on Okinawa, for example, is said to be twice as high as with military base areas outside Japan (Chalmers Johnson, *Blowback: The Costs and Consequences of American Empire*, 2000).

This lenient approach to occupation is a remarkable contrast with the cruel military campaigns the United States conducted during the war, and I don't mean only the atomic bombs they dropped on Hiroshima and Nagasaki. The

US Air Force, you see, targeted not only military facilities but also civilians in most major cities, who were mostly women, children and the elderly (young and middle-aged men were all in military service). Pilots dropped unused bombs on isolated islands with no military significance whatsoever on their way back to their bases, since the Japanese Air Force was powerless by then and no danger of retaliation existed. The pilots appeared to be having fun doing so. No one else has ever killed the enemy's civilians on such a scale. As I will reiterate later, the United States had insisted on fighting till Japan surrendered unconditionally, even after Germany had fallen. Such an insistence would naturally invite desperate attempts from the opponent, adding casualties on both sides. It is difficult not to see a certain cruelty in the way the US military fought—to go all the way till it knocked the enemy down utterly and completely. War is war, one might say, but the degree of cruelty demonstrated is beyond such rationalization.

Broad-minded US occupational policies toward Japan, I believe, were related to the cruelties they had demonstrated toward the end of the war; it was a reaction or a compensation. Americans have their own set of principles and would not easily succumb to apologizing, but they, with human hearts, must have felt guilty for having dropped the atomic bombs. It was extremely unsettling, I would think, not to do anything about such guilt. Another reason for leniency, of course, was the Cold War, which began shortly after the occupation started, making it advantageous for the United States to keep Japan on its side. There is yet another factor which I will discuss later. In any event, lack of resistance among the Japanese toward occupation can be explained in part by American broad-mindedness.

It is peculiar, nonetheless, that the Japanese have shown so little resistance to American control not only during the occupation but in the years to come. They accepted the occupation with a degree of submissiveness rarely seen in their history. So much so that objective or rational explanations, such as that the Japanese military was atrocious and US occupation was lenient, do not seem to be sufficient. What we see here, in my opinion, is a kind of reaction that is not altogether rational. It is a phenomenon of self-delusion, and this time the delusion points in the opposite direction from that earlier one that encouraged the Japanese to go to war with America. As I will discuss in the following chapter, people in Japan are suffering from this self-delusion even today.

Chapter Three

Stockholm Syndrome

Looking at the relationship between Japan and the United States in the modern era, we find a few phenomena never seen previously. The war between the two nations saw soldiers who seemed to be eager to die, who were willing to give their lives in suicidal missions (although some, no doubt, were forced via mass psychology) for the first time in Japanese history. Both the dropping of atomic bombs and air raids of a massive scale on enemy civilians were what the American military had done for the first time in its history. Similarly, military occupation with such a lenient approach was not seen before; so was the readiness of the people to follow its rule. All of these impress me as peculiar—a mystery, which I propose we should try to understand more fully.

A SCHIZOPHRENIC STATE

It is my theory that modern Japan has been psychologically split, like a schizophrenic patient, between two forces: one is what I call the "outer self," which is humble, ready to bend, and admires the West, and the other, the "inner self," which is megalomaniac and despises, as well as is hostile to, the West. The suicidal behavior of soldiers unwilling to be captured, kamikaze pilots ready to die for a larger cause, and the view, entertained by some historians, that Japan is a divine nation are all tied to the force of Japan's inner self. The outer self, on the other hand, has demonstrated itself in the manner in which the dictates of the Occupational Government were followed, as well as in what is generally referred to as "a self-persecutory view of history." I see this split as a social pathology. Neither side has a clear objective nor rationale, and the shifts—from the outer to the inner self, and from the inner to the outer self—are so abrupt that one has to consider them unnatural and irrational.

Of these two, the shift from the inner to the outer self can be interpreted as a case of so-called Stockholm Syndrome, a term derived from a bank robbery that took place in Stockholm during the 1970s. People taken as hostages on that occasion were reported to be unresistive to their captors. Not only did they not attempt to rescue themselves, they also exhibited no behavior expected under such a circumstance. Hostages appeared sympathetic, even respectful, toward their captors; a few even volunteered to keep a watch on police activities, and when the police finally broke into the bank, others tried to save the robbers from being captured.

This type of peculiar and mysterious behavior is found elsewhere. Patricia Hearst, heir of an American media mogul who had been kidnapped earlier, suddenly surfaced as an active participant in a bank robbery, taking the world by surprise; it was apparent that she wasn't under any threat of force at that time. In Japan, too, a similar incident took place in 1968, when Hi Ro Kim, a native of Korea (who, having finished his prison term, was sent back to Korea), took thirteen hostages for four days in Fujimiya Inn at Sumatakyo Hot Springs Resort on the upper Ohigawa River. Here again, hostages showed their respect and trust toward Kim, and one of them, who had been released to go on some errand, refused to take that chance and escape: "I've got to act honorably," this man is said to have announced, and went right back to the room to join the other hostages. A well-known incident, in which a Japanese officer, a POW, got into an American combat plane and directed the pilot to proper targets (Iwakawa Takashi, *A Critical Moment*, 1984) is also an example of Stockholm Syndrome. As in other cases (and to the amazement of the American bomber pilot), this sublieutenent volunteered his service.

As is schizophrenic disorder, Stockholm Syndrome can be observed in those who are placed in highly critical conditions, where safety is not guaranteed unless they engage in certain actions against their will, a situation where keeping luxuries (such as pride, integrity, belief and ideology) would lead to death, while abandoning them might assure survival. If the situation is not very serious, one can deal with it without too much difficulty. But there are times when it is bad enough, and as we face the life and death circumstance, we tend to escape into denial and self-delusion.

The mechanism of schizophrenia has yet to be totally understood, but one theory explains that it is caused by early relationships with one's parents. Suppose a child is raised by parents who neither love nor understand him, but instead force their own selfish demands upon him. He does not want to comply with such demands, but not doing so would invite parental abandonment, while compliance brings care and protection. Considerable psychological strength is required for any child to see that his parents' demands are against his own will. It is not easy to recognize first that his true desire, his inner self, if you will, is in conflict with such demands and then to decide to comply, keeping a clear view as to the reasons for the decision. Not many children have such strength. Unable to sustain the tension, as well as the conflicts and anxiety, most of them would try to bend their will and give up their desires. In other words, they would deny their inner self and resort to repression. They would try to see that their parents' demands are their own by deluding themselves. Then, their conflicts become invisible from the outside. The part of the child that goes along with parental demands is the outer self, and the child might live with it for many years, clinging to a false sense of security.

The child's repressed inner self, however, hasn't vanished. It remains in the realm of the unconscious, being disconnected from the exterior, the real world. The inner self in such a state is damaged; not being healthy, it has invited in all sorts of fantasies and unconscious materials. The child's ego, now altered, or warped, is delusory. One day, usually during the post-adolescence, this repression reaches its limit and the inner-self comes out—bursting and breaking the wall, as it were. Although the child sees it as his true self, this self is not what parents expect or hope to see, and, as it is delusory, it appears as though the child has gone mad. This, some explain, is the mechanism behind schizophrenic onset.

Stockholm Syndrome is not based, as schizophrenia is, on childhood experiences and relationships with parents, but the mechanism is the same. When we talk about schizophrenia, we are looking at the point of time when the repressed inner-self bursts out, but Stockholm Syndrome is a phenomenon seen at the time when the new outer-self is shaped by repressing the inner-self. Hostages in the Stockholm bank, Patricia Hearst, and those in Sumatakyo Hot Springs Resort, as well as Sublieutenant Miyajima, were all forced into a situation where resisting the captor might endanger their lives (or so they thought). It is humiliating to give in, but not to do so means death. Now, there is a way to get out of this difficult predicament, and that is through denial and self-delusion. By convincing themselves that the choice was their own, that they never had a desire to contradict their captors. In this way, they not only save their lives but also keep their pride intact (although only subjectively because the choice they have made is, objectively speaking, humiliating).

Once such a delusory state is established, it has to stay on so that a repressed sense of humiliation will not return. Furthermore, even when the real danger is removed, one cannot suddenly stop deluding oneself. Patricia Hearst must have hated her terrorist kidnappers and didn't want to give in at first. Groups like her kidnappers usually have some kind of rationale to justify their conduct (such as "for the good of the people" and "to correct evil," or that robbing a bank is necessary to secure funds), and Ms. Hearst accepted her kidnappers and their rationales, to which she held on as her lifeline. She must have reasoned that she, too, had been aware of many problems of her society, and that she ought to join her kidnappers to solve those problems and bring about a better society. So she persuaded herself to go ahead and cooperate with the terrorists. If she stopped cooperating, she would have to admit to herself that she had discarded her pride in order to protect her life, a humiliating and self-degrading thought. When her life was no longer under threat, or when immediate physical threat was eliminated, she became even more eager to go along with her kidnappers. This is what must have happened to Patricia Hearst when we found her participating in the bank robbery. A similar speculation can be made in the case of Sublieutenant Miyajima.

Self-deception, however, is a deception, no matter how well rationalized. Moreover, when the deceiver and the deceived are the same person, unlike in the case where one is deceived by someone else, the fact of deception is recognizable only to that person. Repression eliminates original humiliation, but that doesn't mean we are entirely free from it. Not recognizable as such, the humiliation does remain as an uncomfortable feeling. Not seeing things that are there, not knowing the knowable, and not feeling things that clearly exist is altogether possible for any one of us. We are capable of deceiving ourselves because our psyche provides many subtle mechanisms for doing so. There are many examples of this in our daily lives: cancer patients may think they are doing well while somewhere in their minds they know otherwise, or a couple who somehow know their relationship is at a dead end may talk themselves into thinking it isn't.

It is most likely that both Patricia Hearst and Sublieutenant Miyajima had fallen into this kind of deception, and deep down in their minds, they knew they did not agree with their enemies. It was a forced conversion that they had experienced, and it was naturally problematic. Although it would have to be stopped sooner or later, they meanwhile did their best to keep on deceiving themselves and resist chances that might cause them to give up self-deception. Once the deception is broken down and eliminated, however, they would find it extremely difficult to understand their own previous thoughts and actions.

PRICE OF DECEPTION

In the way Japan has been relating to the United States since the end of the Pacific War I see the same pattern of behaviors observed in Patty Hearst and Sublieutenent Miyajima. I might say, therefore, it is a case of large-scale Stockholm Syndrome that Japan suffers as a nation. I cannot find any other way to explain the dramatic turnaround and shift from "fighting on the home front" and "hundred millions of us all go broke" to acquiescence to the occupation and eager acceptance of American ideas in political as well as educational systems, and of the American way of life. Such a turnaround is what we see in the cases of Stockholm Syndrome as well as in schizophrenic patients with confusion between their inner and outer selves. Japan's post-war phenomenon has too many elements that are illogical, irrational and self-deceptive. As we know, Sublieutenant Miyajima was not the case of a crazy man. He was the forerunner of all the Japanese who have come to welcome occupational troops, accepting and admiring their culture and ideas in the name of democracy. He was merely a bit ahead of the time.

Although I find Japanese phenomena pathological both right before and after the war, the latter, in my opinion, is a more severe case. Today there are many people who are eager to list Japan's wrongdoing in the pre-war era and they do not realize how illogical they are, that they are under the influence of self-deception. Here are some examples of the statements that reveal the state they are in: people had opposed the war but were dragged into it by military bullies; losing the war was actually good for Japan, since this helped it overcome militaristic nationalism and become a democratic nation; theJapanese Constitution, with its renunciation of all wars, is the model for the rest of the world. By proposing that these opinions are the outcome of self-deception, I may sound as if I am defending a right-wing ideology and jingoistic nationalism (both of which have gained popularity in Japan in more recent years), but what I want to say is simply that Japan both before and after the war is pathological. Only the mechanism behind the pathology points in diametrically opposite directions. No other propositions are intended.

Let's now take the issue of the ninth article of Japan's Constitution, which renounces all wars. I don't necessarily object to this article, but I do propose, as others have, to rewrite the Constitution and put in it the same renouncement. In other words, I don't side with those who insist that the Constitution, even though it was forced upon us, is fine because its content is just. That is a kind of argument belonging to people who have lost self-respect. It is the thought of a servile person and it resembles that of a raped woman who argues against herself and says, for example, that having carefully guarded her worthless virginity was wrong, or that sex is important to her, and the rapist has opened a door to a more fulfilling life. Something is clearly wrong with this woman's logic and if she doesn't see it, it is because she has lost her self-respect. To say about the Constitution that what matters is the content and how we have gotten it makes no difference is analogous to saying that whether one gets food with the money earned by working or through prostitution, or by begging on the street, makes no difference because the food is equally nutritious.

Doesn't this logic remind us of the way some revolutionary parties justify violence as a tactic, and of the people who insist that the end justifies the means? In these arguments, violence is a necessary evil to reach a just society. But the regime established through violence will have no choice but to maintain it with violence, and revolutionary governments can eventually become totalitarian regimes worse than those against which they have rebelled. A just end does not justify unjust means, but rather, unjust means will corrupt a just end. As ends and means are both parts of an organic whole, one cannot separate the two; we cannot reach the just by employing wrong means. Pacifism handed down by someone else is false pacifism, which is fragile and can be easily corrupted. Looking at its exterior may not tell, but how one has obtained it makes a difference.

I will now go back to the example of a raped woman, so bear with me. Rape, we tend to think, is perpetrated by a stranger on a dark street at night. Studies show, however, that in many cases the rapist is someone known to the victim. When a woman is raped by a man close to her, the common reaction is to deny the fact of rape at first, particularly if she is a virgin. Psychological mechanism of this denial is easy to understand. Since rape is humiliating, or, since it is too painful to accept that a first sexual encounter was disastrous, the woman may resort to denial. She may rationalize that it was in fact she who let it happen, that she actually wanted it to happen. She may force herself to believe what is not true, and soon, the rape becomes consensual sex. This, of course, is the result of self-deception. In order to hold on to the illusion she herself has created, furthermore, she may even volunteer to have sex with the rapist. She has to prove to herself that she actually loves him, or, that sex is very important for her. (If a raped woman has sex of her free will after the incidence, I've heard, the court does not consider the first encounter as rape. This seems to reveal poor understanding of rape victims' psychology, since it is the rape that has made a woman vulnerable and willing to become further involved.) Even if a raped woman were to succeed in denying the fact of rape, she is not free from the sense of humiliation that comes from being forced, and she may not be able to enjoy sex afterwards. Piled up self-disgust may one day burst, causing her to rebel or run away from her partner.

Suggesting that the way Japan behaves in relating to America is analogous to that of a raped woman is not so ludicrous as it may seem. In fact, the two are very similar. Japan was raped, as it were, first by Commodore Perry, then by General MacArthur. While having tried to deny it, Japanese leaders did recognize somewhat accurately what had occurred on the first occasion. The "friendship" treaty forced upon Japan eventually broke down. On the second occasion of rape, however, the Japanese convinced themselves that it was consensual. Having gone back to the prior "friendship" relationship with the United States, they are now firmly resolved to maintain it.

But if this resolve is based on self-deception, we have a problem; we should be concerned about the danger of breakdown, too. One can hardly deny that Japan is in a self-deceptive mode in relating to the United States, ever since the end of the Pacific War. Officially, the two nations are "equal" and close partners, but the Japanese people somehow know that their country is a tributary of the United States. They are aware that the state of occupation continues.

We tend to hold onto our pride even when it is false and precariously hanging in the air. We may also deny certain facts while admitting them to be true somewhere in our mind. This knowledge reveals itself in our actions and attitudes, which, without confidence, are not convincing. Without realistic and rational judgments, behaviors are haphazard; they cannot be otherwise. Japan's relationship with the United States has been, and still is, like this. See, for example, the way the Japanese react on occasions when Americans behave badly on their soil. Anger is usually withheld, and if shown, it is expressed hesitantly, even fearfully; often, people merely go through the motions. When Japanese girls were raped by American Marines, people were outraged but did not pursue justice. Their anger was halted somewhere in the air. The Japanese know that the United States is their boss, and Japan, as its henchman, cannot complain too much.

During the Gulf War, you recall, the Japanese government first offered four billion dollars to aid the war, and when urged to give more, added another nine billion. I don't have a very clear sense how much 13 billion dollars is, but it is not a small amount (someone told me it is something like ten thousand people spending ten thousand yen dining and wining every night for forty years). The way the Japanese government handled this matter involving huge amount of money was disgraceful, to say the least. It was as if the money were handed grudgingly as the United States told Japan what to do, and Japan couldn't refuse. You might also recall that some Japanese were sympathetic to the Iraqis, with whom they apparently identified psychologically. They said they were reminded of their own country during the war under the United States' mighty military power. Deep down, many Japanese weren't eager to cooperate with America, but Japan's economy depends on oil from the Middle East, and US intervention was necessary to secure that oil. Not to cooperate was impossible. This flagging state of mind was reflected in the governmental action, and the American must have felt disappointed, indeed. Who would want to be thankful for cooperation given half-heartedly ? In my opinion, this episode negatively affected the US administration, making it not want to take Japan seriously—the nation without principles, and with people who would only give upon urging. If Japan had offered the fund without being asked, the 13 billion dollars would have gone a long way, but it turned out to be a total waste. When the Gulf War was over and the Kuwaiti government expressed gratitude to those nations who offered their support, Japan was not on the list. America made a fool out of Japan, Iraq was mad, and Kuwait ignored Japan. In the end, no one was pleased.

This disaster was inevitable because Japan is not sure where she stands in her relationship with the United States, and because she is deceiving herself, acting as if she is not America's henchman. If Japan did not belong to the United States, you see, she wouldn't have had to necessarily offer the money. Japan could have refused on the ground that the war was started without prior agreement and that it was an American war. If the government actually made such a statement, it would have been applauded by those who deny that Japan is America's henchman. But the government didn't have the guts to go that far; it had to consider the aftermath of such a daring act. So, Japan gave the money. It couldn't be helped, was the conclusion. It was a fiasco that went very poorly, I must say.

If Japan sees clearly where she stands in her relationship with the United States, then there is little problem in identifying what her role is and what obligations she has. She can see the limits beyond which she is not responsible. When Japan denies reality and says that she is not America's henchman, while deep down realizing otherwise, the result is ambivalent actions and moods. A rational mind sees certain actions as necessary, but a sense of humiliation makes Japan refuse such actions. When Japan is required to speak up as a henchman, she does not do so, being unnecessarily fearful or being overly reserved with excess humility. All of these actions would lead to the loss of confidence and the ability to judge, and whichever direction Japan took in this matter, it would not be in accord with reality. It is an inevitable outcome of having closed our eyes to the aspect we don't want to see. Leaders of the Japanese government may think they are doing fine in spite of everything, but what they are doing is merely getting by with some deceptive measures.

It is true that there are times and circumstances when we, either as an individual or a nation, cannot help but feel humiliated. Then we ought to recognize the situation as humiliating and act accordingly. If we delude ourselves into thinking the humiliating circumstance to be something else, and if we rationalize our behavior in the name of love, devotion and loyalty, etc., we cannot judge our reality with cool-headed objectivity. Then, we are unable to eliminate our sense of humiliation, and even when it is no longer necessary to feel humiliated, or when we are able to act independently, we will remain dependent. Not grasping the situation accurately, we will remain fearful and worry about making the boss angry. Even though there are ways to eliminate the fear, we won't be able to find them. It is the same with love between a man and a woman. Even though the relationship has already ended, and even though, say, the woman has the means to live on her own, she may remain fearful and cling to the man. She does not leave her dependent relationship, saying that "true love" is binding her, or rationalizing that "love is blind."

We need to recognize humiliation if we experience it, and we need to grasp all the facts about the reality that has brought it. Only then can we get rid of the sense when reality no longer warrants it. In absence of this recognition the sense of humiliation stays on as an undercurrent, occasionally surfacing and manifesting itself as a hostile rebellion. This rebellion, however, is nothing but a temporary relief, a chance of letting off steam; it is merely a way to relieve anxiety. Not only does it keep the basic problem of dependency unsolved, but such rebellion could make the situation worse.

MANNERS OF SUBMISSION

Japan sometimes behaves toward the United States with meaningless rebellion and resistance, good examples of which were the large-scale demonstrations to block the US-Japan Mutual Security Treaty. Those were quite meaningless, if you ask me. From the US point of view, they were anti-American riots. Although the sentiment of those who participated was exactly that, I wonder how many of the demonstrators shouting for peace and democracy were aware of that fact. When the riots ended as if a tsunami had subsided, there was nothing left to talk about.

We all know how painful it is to acknowledge the fact that we are in a humiliating circumstance. All of us go through experiences that are humiliating one time or another, and the choice open to us then is one of the following: not to lose sight of reality and take practical and effective actions that would lead to solving problems, or to deny reality in order to avoid pain and cling to false pride, as well as the sense of security, via self-deception, which would lead us to an unrealistic and idiotic path. These are the only choices we as an individual or a nation can have, and we know what happens when we ignore reality. To repeat what I've said earlier, the Japanese military campaigns failed because they were carried out ignoring the realities. No matter how desperately the leaders held onto their belief of victory, no matter how much bravery the soldiers who fought displayed, and no matter how much sacrifice they made, defeat was inevitable because of the realties that were ignored.

Whether or not we see reality accurately determines our outcomes. This is true with a nation, or with an individual. Neurosis occurs because a painful or disagreeable reality, such as a parental mistreatment in early childhood, is left unconfronted. When that reality is observed without distortion, neurotic behavior corrects itself. Even if neurosis is cured, however, it doesn't mean we live the rest of our lives happily filled with bliss. In fact, we may feel less happy as we confront a disagreeable reality. But to live means to keep our eyes firmly upon our reality, and it is not so difficult to do so. If we don't do so, we as an individual or a nation will be in trouble sooner or later.

Recognizing the reality of the humiliating relationship with the Unite States and accepting the role as a henchman is an option Japan can take. Independence doesn't have to be the only and absolute goal. To part with the United States does have some demerits economically and militarily. To begin with Japan will become less wealthy. If the decision is to continue to go along with the status quo so that Japan will stay affluent, that is an option, too. If the decision, based upon rational deliberations, is that depending on the United States' military gives Japan an advantage, so be it. I don't think we should necessarily object to such a decision.

In that case, however, the Japanese have to confront themselves willingly with the resulting sense of humiliation. They are not to deceive themselves and say Japan and the United States are equal partners. This choice also means that America, as the boss, could insist on her way in all matters; occasional rapes of Japanese girls by American servicemen, then, becomes something like a necessary expense. And there is also a possibility of Japan being abandoned, not being needed anymore. The boss does not usually think of his subordinate as much as one wishes him to; he is capricious, to say the least. Japan, in other words, has to live with its uncertain and anxiety-ridden state of dependence. While uncertainty, inconvenience and pain from humiliation must be endured, however, it is not wrong for Japan to choose this path so long as its merit is larger than the demerit, and if she can endure being a subordinate. History has seen many small countries survive amidst powerful nations by keeping up good relations. Japan had long been protected by the Sea of Japan and the Pacific Ocean, but with technological advancements in weaponry, this advantage ceased to exist. One might remind oneself of this fact and conclude that it is necessary for Japan to join the small countries.

Even if remaining America's henchman is the choice made after having weighed pros and cons, it doesn't mean Japan must subjugate itself to the United States totally and blindly. It is probably a peculiarly Japanese tendency to believe that the boss-henchman relationship is absolute, that the boss is always right and the henchman must follow the boss's words under any circumstances. Westerners would not approach the boss-henchman relationship with such an emotionally charged attitude of trust, loyalty and dedication. They are more likely to see it as a deal, or a contract. Countries with less power should be able to insist upon their own rights and not necessarily let the powerful dominate. By being clear on its rights and obligations, and by persuading the United States to accept them, Japan, in fact, might chose this option.

If being America's henchman is too humiliating and if the Japanese think it is pride that is the most important for their country, then they should take the other path. They should assess the demerits of leaving America's reign objectively and in a cool-headed calculation; they should not go about it via such tactics as the surprise attack on Pearl Harbor. To say that leaving America's reign is not possible unless Japan has military power compatible to that of the United States, I think, is not rational.

In choosing to leave America's reign, Japan has to first make the United States understand that it is in a humiliating state of dependence. Then make clear its intention of leaving such a state, and begin serious talks with the United States accordingly. The United States is neither unreasonable nor so wicked as not to turn its ear to listen. I believe the United States is aware of the state Japan is in; of the fact the Japanese consider it humiliating. So long as the Japanese themselves choose not to see it as humiliating and are accepting of the status quo without complaints, however, the United States will not bring it up on its own. Nor will she take an understanding posture by saying something like, "Is this OK with you guys?" Bosses usually do not change voluntarily. It is up to the henchman to quit; he has to say so first and get on with the action. If Japan recognizes the reality to be humiliating and begins to work on eliminating it, the United States wouldn't say offhandedly that such a reality doesn't exist.

It doesn't matter which path Japan decides to take so long as the decision is based on an accurate perception of reality. Japan must not force itself to see it is an equal partner of the United States, and it must not delude itself and boast it can win against America. The important thing is to know what actually benefits Japan. To put on a label of either pro- or anti-American and act accordingly is counterproductive.

A type of scolding saying that Japan doesn't have its feet firmly on the ground and it waffles, or that it must do better, is heard all over the country and on all occasions. But even if one were to resolve to do better, determination and confidence cannot be achieved overnight. It takes time. In cases of individuals, unity in personality has to come first, and if conscious and unconscious mind are moving in opposite directions, unity cannot be achieved. One must acknowledge both the inner and the outer self first, seeing both as a part of personality. Unity of personality cannot be realized by denying the part that is actually there simply because it is peculiar, unacceptable or shameful.

Chapter Four

False Pride

Pride is a necessity for human beings to sustain their lives. It is more than something nice to have but which we can live without; it is not merely a luxury that makes us feel better about ourselves. With our instincts no longer intact, we humans need reasons to go on living. While animals don't need it, we cannot do without a sense that our lives have some meaning and we are worthwhile. Pride gives us this sense.

In order to understand how individual personalities are constructed, I find it useful to look at them in terms of what I call "the illusory self" and "the real self." When human babies come into this world, they have neither knowledge nor any abilities. Their instincts, however, are already "broken," no longer entirely intact, and they don't know their realities, since no contact has yet been made. In other words, they live in non-reality, and in this world of non-reality, their "broken" instincts float, unorganized and producing illusions of numerous types. Human babies are in this "narcissistic state" in psychoanalytic theory when they are born. As their sensory and motor functions develop, and as frustrations are experienced, they begin to know the reality that surrounds them (according to "the illusionist theory," the reality they then discover is not reality, but pseudo-reality, but we do not go into this discussion just now).

DISCOVERY OF "THE REAL SELF"

Unlike this illusory world of fantasies into which human babies are born, the real world they come to know is full of impossibility and unwanted things. The fantasy world, where nothing is limited and anything is possible, is a world of seeing everything and knowing all. As reality is introduced and it invades their fantasies, however, the world around them, as well as they themselves, will be split into two—the illusory and the real.

The illusory side of the self is narcissistic, and as it continues to feel omnipotent, one might call it the megalomaniac self. In the real world are "others," however, and these others are unfamiliar to the newcomers, to say the least. The real self, needing to negotiate in this real world, is generally helpless. It is limited, even controlled, by others. It may feel powerless and inferior as well.

When our selves are split into a megalomaniac, knowing-all part on one side and a powerless and inferior part on the other, the two are clearly in opposition. As we grow up and achieve psychological and personality integration, the megalomaniac side will change, becoming less fantastic (there are people who don't perform this task very well and polarized opposition remains, causing symptoms such as manic-depression). These now better-balanced illusions are what we call pride and self-respect. The powerless part of the self will also change, becoming more capable as it gains real-world experience and training; it becomes more realistic. Changes in two sides of our self do not occur, nor complete, at one time. The process is continuous and when shocking incidents or major setbacks are experienced, causing the phenomenon of regression, the illusory part becomes more megalomaniac, while the real part goes down into a less powerful and capable state.

I need to point out here that while the real self reflects our reality more accurately, objectively speaking, it is the illusory self that is more genuine, truer and more natural in our subjective mind. Therefore, we tell ourselves that the illusory self hasn't yet fully realized itself, being blocked by some obstacles but eventually and inevitably it will. We feel this illusory self to be real since we perceive it always being there (when, in the beginning, there is no distinction between the self and the other, we may not want to call it illusory "self"). In contrast, the real self seems to have come from nowhere. It appears to be what we are forced to acknowledge whenever we experience problems or conflicts with other people, something we want to eliminate if we can. As the real self is defined, or forced upon us, by the outsider, in other words, we would rather not believe it to be our self. Compared to the wonderful illusory self, of which we can be proud, it appears insignificant or nothing special.

It would be easier for us to live only with the real self (which, being shaped in the process of going through various relationships with others, naturally functions well in the real world). We would then have less trouble in real life. Because our sense of value and joy of living comes from our illusions, life, then, will be empty, tiresome, and hard to endure, however. If we are to exist only with our illusory self, on the other hand, we will feel good, even euphoric, but such a state does not last. Moreover, by not adjusting to the real world we might not be able to sustain our lives. If we allow the illusory self to take over the real self, in other words, we might have to resort to suicide, with which we eliminate the real self. But we human beings manage to get on with life, balancing inherently conflicting elements of the illusory and the real self.

What I say here about individual human beings can be applied to groups — a nation or an ethnic group. There are no groups or nations without some kind of creation myths or stories about the origin of the founding of their country. It is these stories that provide the race or the nation a sense of value and pride. They are myths, however. Although they contain some elements of which a group or a nation can be proud, they are not very realistic.

Japan's creation myth — stories about the founding of the nation — begins with Izanagi and Izanami and continues to Ninigi no Mikoto (Prince Ninigi), a grandson of Amaterasu. Ninigi no Mikoto has descended from Takamaga-hara (heaven) to Mt. Takachiho in the region of Hyuga. His grandson or great-grandson, the story goes, went to the Yamato region and became Emperor Jinmu, the ruler of the tribe. What this story tells us is that the ancestor of Japan's emperor came from heaven.

The myth of Ninigi no Mikoto has produced various ideas about the Japanese — that they are pure and unique and of a single origin. What we call the Japanese race, however, consists of diverse groups. Some came from Siberia and Sakhalin Island via the Korean Peninsula and others from Southeast Asia and the South Pacific. There was a lot of mixing, but the strongest, or the group with the most in number, was the group from the Korean Peninsula. This group, who had previously controlled both the Peninsula and the chain of islands nearby (*Kudara* and *Wa*), appears to have fought in the latter half of the seventh century (around 663AD) against another group (*Shinra*), which was aided by the Tang court, at a place called Hakusukinoe. The defeated side retreated to an island and there they formed the Yamato court. The myth of heavenly descent, in other words, was created in order to hide the fact that they were a mixed race and they had been defeated and driven from the Korean Peninsula. A story of heavenly descent was created because the people could not be proud of what had actually happened, and needed to hide that incident.

The vanquished in a war were usually reduced to oblivion in those days, but the Japanese race survived because of unusually good luck. For example, they found the chain of islands nearby which provided a safe haven. This might explain a peculiar characteristic commonly seen among the Japanese — the particular fondness they hold for certain historical figures, such as Minamoto Yoshitsune, Kusunoki Masashige, Toyotomi Hideyoshi and Saigo Takamori, all of whom are heroes destined to fail in the end. This propensity to side with the loser over the winner is so peculiar that it makes me wonder if it has something to do with their country's having been formed by heroes who had been defeated. It might be that the Japanese rediscover their primitive selves every time they are defeated.

Amae is another common characteristic among the Japanese. Its existence also points to the now-forgotten past. As explained by Doi Takeo in his *Anatomy of Dependency*, the term refers to a tendency to not want to doubt others, an inclination to be overly and often carelessly trusting. This tendency makes people not to want to confront others and easily succumb to compromises even if it means disregarding rules and principles. Although they are sincere and have a keen sense of duty and obligation, people with *amae* are also inclined to resort to self-deception to save face. These characteristics, I believe, are of those who were defeated and withdrew into a well-protected place — like the Japanese archipelago. Gregory Clark, who described Japan as "a large tribal village," has a point: if a group of people with *amae* mentality had found themselves somewhere on a continent — near China, Europe, or the Middle East — they would have been obliterated in no time. In such a place, where various different races struggle to survive, people with a trusting nature and a need for mutual dependency could not survive.

Westerners find *amae* dependency unacceptable because such tendencies (as described above) are usually found in psychological maladjusted individuals. They find it hard to believe that the Japanese, seemingly well-adjusted people, have such needs. The Japanese, in turn, should realize that *amae* is not universal, that it can be found only in certain special circumstances. To side-track a bit, I often wonder what the Japanese are going to do with the characteristics I mention here. When they were able to stay by themselves and relate only among themselves, there was little problem; but how will they manage in this age when that option is becoming increasingly difficult? Perhaps there's no need to worry because as they encounter troubles, get hurt and learn, this tribal characteristic will change.

In any event, Japan's first emperor was most likely not someone who had militarily conquered the people inhabiting the islands. Rather, he was chosen as the leader of various groups who united their forces under the threat of a Tang-Shinra takeover, and opted to support the Yamato court. He was, in other words, the result of, in today's term, *dango*, a method of selecting leadership practiced even today in all types of organizations. As the Yamato court tried to emulate the Tang Dynasty in legal and land ownership systems, among others (although emulating didn't work very well, as the social conditions between the two were quite different), however, the emperor was also to be like the Tang's. The myth of the Emperor Jimmu was thus born, and he was supposed to have conquered the land by force.

Creating an emperor identical to that of a powerful enemy to make the people believe in the power they did not possess at the point of an imminent threat was to be repeated during another time of crisis. At the time of the Meiji Restoration (which restored the rule of the emperor), authority resembling that of the absolute God, a belief held by Western nations, was bestowed on the Emperor Meiji. As was the case with the Yamato leadership, people were persuaded that the Emperor Meiji was sacred and absolute.

Shortly after the shattering defeat in the war with the United States, I remember that a theory called "conquering by the nomads" (Egami Namio, *Kibaminzoku kokka* (*The Nation of the Nomads*) became extremely popular among the Japanese. Expounding the myth of the Emperor Jimmu's eastward advance, this theory proposed that the Yamato rulers had taken all the regional powers under their control with their cavalry forces. No doubt followers of this theory imagined that their ancient ruler had conquered their enemies on the Pacific islands, defeating them just as the US military forces did. What they wanted to think was that their defeated nation had once been as powerful as America.

In psychoanalytic theory, the mechanism of trying to overcome fear by imitating a powerful enemy, as in the three examples I've given, is called "identification with the aggressor," and that of repeating past patterns, "compulsive repetition." Psychoanalysis is a theory to explain mechanisms of illusions existing behind behaviors and actions of an individual, but history, which after all is shaped by individual people who have various illusions, is destined to be influenced by them as well. The theory, in fact, is helpful in understanding our histories.

A WISH TO RECOVER THE LOST GROUND

Back to the story of the Yamato, whose origin, I suspect, was in the Korean Peninsula, and whose leaders tried to imitate the Tang dynasty. The story which was created to hide the facts about themselves, and eventually became a myth was that they were unified by the gods descended from heaven. These gods had nothing to do with the people of the Korean Peninsula and China, thus the race of Yamato was pure and unique. This fantasy had to be formed to help the people to go through various crises, but in this fantasy there was obvious self-deception, the outcome of which can be found in many invented stories: that Empress Jinko tried to conquer Korea three times; that the Yamato court had a colony, something like a local agency, in the southern part of the Korean Peninsula, etc. The existence of these unsubstantiated stories is meaningful in itself, but the Japanese seem to be particularly fond of them, and I wonder why.

When there was a chance, or when they had a surplus of wealth and power, it is true, Japanese rulers attempted to advance and invade the Korean Peninsula, as well as the continent beyond. Toyotomi Hideyoshi actually sent soldiers to Korea twice, once in the Bunroku era, and again in the Keicho era (in the sixteenth century). His ambition, it has been said, was to go to China as well. In the modern era, Japan colonized Korea and invaded China. Various theories have been offered to explain the motivation for these occasions, but in my interpretation, it reflected the same dream of going to the continent. The psychological mechanism on both occasions is the same.

Whether merely creating stories or actually carrying them into action, going to Korea and the continent beyond are the result of the same wishful thinking—to recover lost ground. Deep down in the Japanese psyche is a memory of having been driven from the Korean Peninsula, and it was a humiliating and traumatic experience which the people tried to deal with by creating a myth. In other words, they tried to delude themselves while also taking some action. When Japan annexed Korea in 1910, unity between "the inside" (Japan) and "the outside" (Korea) was required, with the result of forcing the Koreans to adopt Japanese names, as well as to worship the Japanese emperor and Shinto shrines. In other words, an attempt was made to make the Koreans into Japanese. This was a very poor and ineffective way to rule a colony; it merely increased hostility among the Koreans, who, with their strong Confucian background, cherished their own ancestors. The question is then why the Japanese carried on such a foolish idea, a notion no one has entertained in the entire history of colonization (the British certainly did not think of trying to make the people of India like themselves). It was because, I think, that their ancestors (who were still Koreans then) had been defeated by other tribes and had to leave the Peninsula and form their own nation elsewhere. It was a sense of retribution that made the people of the Yamato deny Korean values.

The Yamato tribe, in other words, were the Koreans who now wanted to deny their origin. With their true motivation of retribution buried somewhere deep in their minds, the Japanese rulers talked themselves into believing that their colonial policies were good for the Korean people, and Japan should be thanked. Unlike the British who exploited colonized subjects as slaves, they argued, the Japanese were kind, treating the Koreans as their equals and accepting them as Japanese. Seeing it differently, Korean people held a strong hatred of the Japanese. Their bitterness, in fact, surpassed that of the Indians after their independence from British rule. It was bitterness a degree rarely seen among colonized people (Irish resentment toward the English is similarly deep and strong, but the situation is different since England still keeps a part of Ireland as its colony). This was because the Koreans were not only mistreated and exploited (although expenditures being greater than gains, Japan's control over Korea is said to have been economically unprofitable) but humiliated, with their pride deeply damaged. Although the Japanese looked down on the Koreans, the Koreans had long considered the Japanese inferior and they were outraged over being controlled by people they considered inferior. (Just as the French and the Germans seem to have done to each other, neighbors tend to want to see the other as inferior.) While material losses can be forgotten easily, the damage done to our pride is not. It is our human nature.

The reason I focus so much on self-deceptions found in Japan's past, its national and racial origin in particular, is because I look at them with psychoanalytic theory in mind. Psychoanalysis tries to explain the mechanism of early childhood traumas or shocks which would later result in various symptoms such as obsessions, perversions and complexes, and influence personality formation. It also tries to remedy neurosis as well as mental and personality disorders. The mechanism of certain types of disorders—compulsive neurosis or hysteria, which Freud treated, for example—is fairly simple. The cause can be found almost always in the hiding of the facts existing in painful experiences and in the trauma rooted in problematic relationships with parents and/or sexual, as well as physical, violations. Freud defined hysteria as an illness in reminiscence; the etiology is the warping of the past. In other words, self-deception is the cause of the illness.

The principle in treating neurosis, therefore, is very simple: to help the patient to give up and release the repression; to make him bring facts into broad daylight and accept them as they are. By acknowledging the trauma and letting the conflict around it come out of the realm of the unconscious and be placed under the control of the conscious mind, the illness can be cured. Easy to say, but not so in practice, however. For example, admitting the fact of parental violation means for the patient to acknowledge that his parents did not love him, and if that is the case, his ego, built on his belief in parental love, might collapse. So does the fort he has built around himself. If he continues hiding the fact, on the other hand, behavioral symptoms will persist. Being kept in the realm of the unconscious, the past continues to exert its control.

This mechanism of our individual psyche can be applied to a group of people such as a nation or a race, and by so doing we can understand the warp, as it were, existing in that group. If we understand why such a warp has been formed, we will find ways to overcome symptoms, such as failures to make decisions, or making foolish decisions in dealing with other countries. What I am suggesting here is that the method used to treat individual pathologies can be applied to a nation. The first step of the treatment is, as I have done above, to disclose the deception found in the telling of the nation's or the group's origin.

Japan, of course, is not an exception, and other countries have their own pathologies. With their revolutions, which are something like sudden symptomatic eruptions, France and Russian are in my mind more serious cases (I am well aware of the enormous complexity of these revolutions; I also don't want to deny the fact that ideas such as basic human rights or the right to rebel are the outcomes of these revolutions). Modern France fluctuated between a republican system and dictatorship, prolonging its political confusion (for example, Napoleon was made the emperor only eleven years after the people put Louis XVI under the guillotine). This fluctuation was an attempt to rationalize their revolution; one for which the people paid too great a price for what they got.

I maintain that the Japanese empire and the regime in the Soviet Union both lasted for about seventy years, and shared similar structural characteristics as nations that entered the modern world with an inferiority complex toward the Western powers. If I were to extend my theory further, China's political ideology also belongs to the realm of pathology. Because, as Okada Hidehiro said, the Hang race existed only subjectively. As is the case with Japan's myth of heavenly descent, it is megalomaniac. The Chinese considered inhabitants of the continent's peripheries barbarians, but the Hang themselves, you see, had once been barbarians before they integrated themselves into the Hang civilization. In other words, by forgetting their origin they became the Hang. The same with the Japanese. They became the race of the Yamato by forgetting their origin; that they had been the Ezos and Kumasos; that they had been the Northerners—the Korean and the Chinese—, as well as people from South Pacific and Southeast Asia.

No nation can do without a creation myth or a story about its origin and the founding of the nation. Even a new country like the United States had to make up a myth. The Puritans who came to the New World on the Mayflower, in 1620, looking for freedom of religious belief and to build God's country are called Pilgrim Fathers, you see. But that these "Fathers" built the foundation of the United States as a free and democratic country is a myth; it is merely a story about the founding of the country. Some of the Pilgrims certainly came for religious freedom, and it is true that the agreement drawn on the Mayflower included some new and idealistic principles, as well as rules for how to conduct themselves in the new land. What is also true, however, is that some of these people became murderers and killed the native inhabitants who had helped them to settle in an unfamiliar environment. The American story of nation building does not touch upon this and other disgraceful facts, of course, but the problem is that this myth worshipped murderers. So long as it is believed and propagated, this myth is going to be problematic, because then all other killings of enemy alien races cannot be halted. Just as an individual who has repressed unwanted facts of his childhood and created a false story or a warped image about himself is likely to suffer from a mental disorder of some kind, Americans, who made up a story that is not entirely true, experienced various problems in their history, which not only negatively affected other countries, but themselves as well.

A nation, like an individual, needs to believe that its existence is legitimate and that it is worthwhile. In order to do so, it has to have pride. But if they dig far enough into their past, most countries, the powerful and the advanced in particular, will find various elements of which they can't be proud, or something shameful or humiliating about which they feel guilty. They tend to hide these elements and create a story that is more convenient. You may say that those are merely stories and that how they are told is unimportant. But how one recognizes one's past is very important, because we humans live on stories. I will discuss more about the problems America faces later.

FAMILY STORIES

"Family romance" is the name with which Freud has referred to the phenomenon of young children's making up a story which they believe. That, for example, they are of noble stock, but a certain circumstance requires them to be the offspring of an ordinary man and woman like their parents. Both Japan's myth of heavenly descent and that of the Pilgrim Fathers can be seen as a "family romance," a story. We can feel good about ourselves so long as we believe in these stories, but the price we pay for that is not small. The more unrealistic and megalomaniac the story is, the higher the price.

When a schizophrenic patient insists that he is Napoleon, he is not joking. He has to hold onto this megalomaniac idea because otherwise his ego, under some kind of threat, could not sustain itself. This man, in other words, is in some kind of situation that overwhelms him and he needs to fortify his ego. Since no one treats him as normal, however, his mental state will further deteriorate. Japan before the defeat in the war with the United States was in a situation similar to that of this man. As I remember, our primary school history textbook began with the story of heavenly descent. It was also filled with megalomaniac views about emperors, as well as statements like: "Japan is a divinely protected nation as revealed in *kamikaze* (the divine wind) that has prevented the Mongolian armies from invading," or "Japan has never been defeated in war because it belongs to the gods" (as if defeat in Hakusukinoe did not exist), and "as the Japanese military has had no conquerors, Japan has never been colonized" (as if the Meiji government didn't accept unequal treaties pushed by the Western powers).

Some people now ridicule Japan's megalomania of that era, but I myself have some mixed feelings about it. Just as I don't want to do so with schizophrenic patients, I don't want to laugh at the megalomania of Imperial Japan, even though I have deep regret and shame for the harm and pain the people of neighboring countries had to suffer because of it.

But Japan was defeated and its megalomaniac pride was crushed. Because the pride on which the country stood was false, it was quickly trampled. The people then rushed, it seems, to the opposite direction, to an overly self-deprecating state after the war. This state allowed a particular view which, because it has a basis in the outcome of the Tokyo War Tribunal, might be called a "masochistic view of history." It is diametrically opposite to that entertained before and during the war, when national pride was quite megalomaniac. The Japanese had once been forced to embrace, even risk their lives, for such megalomaniac pride previously, and the sacrifices people had made were so great (many Japanese in fact were relieved to see the end of the war) that the common reaction to it was to run to the other extreme.

An attempt to describe post-war Japan according to the outcome of the Tokyo War Tribunal doesn't seem to render an accurate understanding of history, however. By choosing not to recognize some important facts, or by denying some aspects, this view doesn't allow an accurate reflection on reality as it was. Moreover, I find the basic orientation of this position not so different from the pre-war megalomaniac view of Japan.

A self-deprecating view that reflects the outcome of the Tokyo War Tribunal, which said that Japan was wrong in all and every aspect, was widespread during the post-war era. In more recent years we have seen a new trend, which we might call a reaction to the previous reaction. Emergence of this new trend makes me feel cautious, since Japan may be experiencing yet another swing. As I have said earlier, having a split between the illusory and the real self is characteristic of an undeveloped ego. Perhaps it is not easy to position ourselves right at the middle, maintaining a good balance between the two. But, are there only two ways in which Japan can chose its direction— either to insist on megalomaniac pride or to be overly self-deprecating? I don't think that is the case.

These two are both extremes, you see, and are based on one fixed notion that says having pride is not possible unless one has a special ability or has accomplished something extraordinary or mysterious in nature that doesn't allow others to share. If we define pride as such, the only way to have it, one would have to say, is by ignoring reality and living in an illusory world. Because special abilities or extraordinary accomplishments rarely exist in our real world, what is left for us, then, is either to hold megalomaniac pride by disregarding reality, or to fall into self-deprecation without the sufficient support such pride would need.

Instead of trying to find sources of pride in various unrealistic notions, the Japanese people ought to find their pride in their real history and in various aspects of their country as it actually is. If they do so instead of wavering between megalomania and self-deprecation, they will be more motivated to make Japan a country of which they can be genuinely proud. That would be a more realistic goal.

Think of the case with us as individuals, which is the same as for countries and groups. It is entirely wrong to say that unless we are of unique value we are not worth anything. How ridiculous it is to think that only those with special talents, extraordinary abilities, or heroic inclinations, or those with a prestigious family background, have a right to live. Ordinary people with no special talent to speak of have the same right to live, and people who don't agree with this view haven't freed themselves from early childhood narcissism, for whom nothing outside of their narcissistic system is worthwhile. Their life is like that of a man who is fixated on his rigid image of the ideal woman. He thinks no one is suitable for him and will end his life without a single experience with a real woman. What this man has is clearly an illusion which has nothing to do with reality. Individuals, as nations, will have a major problem if they are to look for sources of their pride in something that doesn't exist.

Ordinary people ought to be able to feel proud of being ordinary. There is no need for us to do anything special to prove we are worthwhile. The history of modern Japan, however, didn't follow this path. She instead believed she had to be special. It is understandable that Meiji leaders felt they had to try hard in getting rid of the sense of humiliation caused by what I call the American rape. People had gone too far in conjuring up and maintaining false pride, however. Thus they ended up believing that they had to fight the fatal war with the United States.

Chapter Five

Deceptions Found
in Japanese Pacifism

Having sacrificed many lives, Imperial Japan was dissolved at the end of the Pacific War and Japan became a nation advocating pacifism. "Be a Switzerland of Asia," American General Douglas MacArthur is reported to have said to the Japanese as he landed in the occupied land. He didn't say this because he cherished peace, of course. As we would soon find out in his advocacy of dropping atomic bombs on China during the Korean War, he was among the most hawkish of the career military men. What kind of man was he, you might wonder, preaching an ideal he didn't believe in? What he meant to say probably was that Japan should forever give up any thought of fighting with the United States. Japan's post-war pacifism was thus created by the push from the United States.

CONCEPTUALIZING PEACE

Japan's losses in the war with the United States were huge. The lives of 3.1 million people including all those who died in the Greater East Asian War (but most of these deaths were in the war against the United States) were lost. American losses did not seem so great from the Japanese point of view—relatively small casualties of 50,000 (320,000, if one also includes those lost in Europe), with no bombing of their homeland. But the war was a major blow for Americans as well. Even before the war ended, therefore, their leaders had began thinking of ways to prevent future Japanese hostility against their country. The way the US forces fought the war with unprecedented cruelty, killing both soldiers and civilians indiscriminately (not to mention the two atomic bombs dropped), illustrates this resolution. Their military exercises were to send a clear message that America was not to be slighted and that no one should forget what it would be like to make her an enemy.

Pushing pacifism onto the Japanese was a part of this resolution. In fact, the occupational government showed a great deal of interest, excessive it seemed, in eliminating the elements that might encourage the general population with the idea of retribution, as well as the spirit of fighting back. For example, a stage production of *Tales of Forty-seven Samurai* was prohibited, as the story might stir up a mood of revenge. Also banned were movies of samurai sword fighting—that of Araki Mataemon, for example. The original story of Araki Mataemon involves revenge, killing single-handedly thirty-six samurais to avenge his brother-in-law. When a new version of this story was made into a movie under the occupational government's supervision, it had an altered plot: Mataemon agonizes over what is required of him as a samurai in order to re-store honor, and in the end he kills only one of his brother-in-law's enemies to bring the matter to an end. I know these cases well because my folks owned a movie theater in those days. I was a high school student then, and extra-curricular school activities in martial arts, such as *kendo* and *judo*, were also banned by order of the occupational headquarters.

This enforced pacifism affecting theaters, movies and students' activities was presented to the world as the position Japan had chosen on its own; the will of the general populace. Here, I see a phenomenon of self-deception. I have already talked about this self-deception in reference to the ninth article of the Japanese Constitution (on renouncing all wars), using an analogy of a raped woman, but I will examine it here again, as I believe this issue of self-deception is a crucially important factor in understanding Japan today.

First, I want to make one point very clear. Even though I believe Japan's post-war pacifism was pushed by the US government, I am not against paci-fism itself. I do not worship war. Wars are the greatest folly of all mankind, and peace of course is better than war, but that's not the point here. What I believe should be advocated, however, is a pacifism chosen by free will, not one imposed by someone else. The two are not the same. So long as we be-lieve coerced pacifism is that of one's own choice, we will forever push real pacifism away. Pacifism in a form of self-deception, in other words, is the en-emy of real pacifism. Not earned, but enforced, pacifism will quickly become only an idea, and if it is a mere concept, it leads us neither to the realistic grasping of peace nor to some concrete ways to reach it. It only encourages people to shout for peace. I believe such statements as "we will not take up weapons even against a hostile invasion" or "we will unconditionally oppose any wars" belong to those people who haven't thought how to achieve and maintain peace in concrete ways.

To keep saying that Japan is the only country to have suffered from atomic weapons is fine, but this statement merely says that Japan was a victim. It doesn't give any logical basis for pacifism. Promoting the peace movement as a victim nation may not be a bad approach, but such a strategy probably has little actual power in affecting other nations. It may even give an impression that the Japanese are saying "no more" of those extraordinary experiences and sufferings because they are afraid. Then, outsiders may interpret that Japanese pacifism is based on fear. They may wonder if Japan will discard it once that fear is overcome.

The pacifism found in Japan today is not real pacifism, but something one might call defeatism, or a propensity to surrender. The Japanese accepted the pacifism imposed upon them by America when they lost the war, and they have kept it ever since. Only Japanese people see it as pacifism, but to people elsewhere it comes across as defeatism. No one would believe in such pacifism. If the Japanese pacifist position, which is supposedly on behalf of peace and justice for mankind, turned out to be based on the fear of war, then it is hard for anyone to take the Japanese seriously. In order for the Japanese advocacy for peace to be credible, people must first reject the pacifism that was forced upon them and then create their own, constructing it with their own reasons and rationales.

What the Japanese are practicing today, I might further argue, is a form of masochism. We usually associate masochism with a sexual context, say arousal by whipping or having one's body tied with rope, or by way of some deliberate degradation. But there are other forms of masochism—what Freud called "moral masochism," for example, which is to put oneself in a certain mental situation via self-degradation or self-blame. Motivation behind such a behavior, I think, is an attempt to avoid a sense of humiliation (subjectively, of course, because objectively you will invite more humiliation). In Chapter Three, I explained the mechanism of this avoidance in the cases of schizophrenic disorder and Stockholm Syndrome, but it can be seen also as masochism. Since Japan after the Pacific War is an interesting case of a psychological and psychoanalytical study, I think we should examine it from various angles.

Let's now suppose a tendency commonly found in all of us. When confronted by a strong enemy and when defeat is obvious, we tend to say to ourselves that we didn't care how it ended anyway. Instead of maintaining our resistance against the enemy, we exert our energy to pretend. When we actually face defeat, we make ourselves believe that we had known the outcome all along. Behind this type of masochistic attitude I sense a form of self-delusion. It is an attitude we tend to adopt in order to shield ourselves from the blow of humiliation. By choosing to degrade ourselves, we are putting on a front, as it were, for the enemy to see, and for ourselves to believe that the outcome wasn't forced upon us, that it was actually what we had wanted. It is like retreating twenty steps when only ten are required, in order to show that the retreat was our own choice and not the result of giving in.

Rationalizing defeat in this way inevitably leads us to defeatism along with masochism.

We've heard a great deal of such defeatist argument made among the Japanese public during the post-war era as that it was good for Japan to have lost the war and the defeat had been obvious from the beginning, that the occupational forces freed the Japanese from their own military dictators, although various reforms carried out as the result were in fact what the Japanese had already thought about themselves, and that a new path for pacifist Japan was now paved thanks to the defeat, etc. These types of argument are the product of self-delusion; a feature of moral masochism which was characteristic of the Japanese in the post-war era. Not only did the public depend on this self-delusion, the American occupational government helped to promote it, perhaps realizing its usefulness. General MacArthur, for one, stated that the ninth article of the new Constitution (renouncing any forms of war) was proposed by Kijro Shidehara, then the prime minister, and that he was impressed by Shidehara's enthusiasm and eagerness. This was a lie. The truth was that the Japanese government had resisted the article initially, but resigned to accepting it, realizing the futility of resistance. True, there were many who afterwards felt that the Article Nine was acceptable, even good. Still, it is simply not true that the Japanese proposed it on their own.

When the Japanese people say they want no more wars, that they have learned their lesson, I don't deny they are sincere. But I sense over- zealousness in this kind of statements, making me wonder if their words are to hide their self-deception. You see, many of them actually enjoyed the war for a while. Volunteers to go to China to fight were many, and parades were held everywhere to celebrate the fall of Nanking. People were overjoyed at the news of success in the surprise attack on Pearl Harbor. To say that they were dragged into the war by their military leaders isn't entirely true. No doubt, the war was pushed by the military, but it did so probably because its leaders did not want to lose popular support. Politicians who had tried to avoid the war were put under threat by rightist groups, you see, but those groups were made up primarily of civilian volunteers. Considering all of these, one has to say that Japan at the end of the war was like a person who suffered from amnesia. If this forgetting is not self-delusion, what is?

JAPAN'S "PEACE CONSTITUTION"

Some Japanese have been treating their Constitution as if it is a sacred document. I call them "Constitution fetishists," and I find their rigid attitude pathetic. It reminds me of the pre-war ideology of *kokutai* (state-nationhood, or, in a more contemporary term, national identity). *Kokutai* ideology was to serve the people, you see, but it was made into something of the utmost importance for which people should sacrifice themselves. In fact, many lost their lives for it. It was a fetish idea. But the idea of changing any part of the Constitution, or even bringing the issue up for discussion, has long been taboo in Japan. Although somewhat eased in more recent years, questioning of this taboo is still rejected by those who call themselves the "guardians of the Constitution" (Takako Doi of the Social Democratic Party who has reportedly proclaimed a vow of marriage to the Constitution is an example).

There are people who argue that Japan's so-called Peace Constitution has to be carefully guarded, since it was obtained at the sacrifice of 3.1 million lives during the war. I find this logic problematic, too. A constitution should be evaluated based on the needs of the majority of the people of the time to see whether its desired standards and rules are right for the public to follow. What price one had to pay to get it is irrelevant.

A similar type of argument, you might recall, was used by people who objected to the army's retreat from China during the war. According to Yamamoto Shichihei, withdrawal from the continent was suggested more than once on the basis that there was nothing to be gained, as the war had developed into a mess by then. Every time it was made, however, the proposal met objection based on the same rationalale: the retreat was an affront to the *eirei*, the soul of the dead soldiers. If the Army were to put their weapons down and leave the continent, the objectors maintained, their deaths would become meaningless. Thus retreat was not an option. Their logic, I suppose, was to continue fighting and make more *eirei*.

The Japanese who are proud of their Peace Constitution while advocating the keeping of the Mutual Security Treaty with the United States are equivalent to a greedy money-lender putting up a sign as a philanthropist. A decent person would keep such a sign hidden; he'd maintain a low key about his business. Those who say that they are proud of the Constitution also remind me of a thief who boasts that his family belief is not to lie and not to steal. For the Japanese to say that theirs is a nation of peace-loving people is like a rich man who relies on a gangster (the US military) for his safeguard to announce to the world that he wants to get along with everybody, that he detests quarrels and doesn't believe in violence. This rich man, furthermore, asks the gangster to train his sons (Japan's Self-Defense Force) to improve their skill in fighting. Who would trust a rich man like this?

There are those who rationalize that although they are against the Mutual Security Treaty, it is the government that let the US military lease the land. This type of rationalization resembles politicians whose habit is to excuse themselves by putting blame on their secretaries. It is our votes that elect politicians and shape the government; we are responsible for what our government does.

Being proud of something that was forced upon, or something with no reality to back up, makes Japan look ridiculous as well as difficult to understand. Japan's pacifism, as it is, is hypocrisy at best. I do not necessarily advocate for Japan to be neutral and demilitarized, but if we want to be proud of our Constitution, we have to first achieve neutrality and make other nations recognize it. Laws, including the Constitution, exist for the people, and when they cease to serve the purpose for which they were originally written, we should be able to alter them. Making them an object of admiration, something you want to commit yourself to with devotion and faith, is simply comical. Constitution and *kokutai* fetishism, as well as the fetishism of bravery required of Japanese soldiers, have the same mechanism as that of sexual fetishism, which seeks not a female body and her sexual organs but her underwear, shoes and such in order to be aroused. It is like putting the cart before the horse.

The issues of war and peace are directly related to what kind of nation people want, and I am sure there are many different views on this. Whatever choices are to be made, people should not base their judgment on self-delusion. We need to remind ourselves also that there isn't such a thing as universal truth—that which is true under any circumstances or regardless of who says so and when. The same thing can be true or false depending on the circumstances. A boast made with no one to back it up is the same as a megalomaniac expression of a schizophrenic patient. For our boast to be true, we have to convince others to give us their support. When Napoleon himself says he is Napoleon, there is no delusion, because people around him also see him as Napoleon.

FROM ONE EXTREME TO THE OTHER

It is understandable, one might say, that Japan, having narrowed her vision, let herself go astray and firmly believe in the importance of military strength, that winning wars was the ultimate goal for which anything could be excused. The Japanese (perhaps other people as well) tend to let themselves get bogged down with one idea or another when major setbacks are experienced. Granted, there were reasons, but Japan tried too hard. She budgeted and spent far beyond what she could afford in building up the military and sacrificed the daily lives of her people. When that proved to be insufficient, she then resorted to self-conceit, over-assessing her military power. The notion that Japanese soldiers are unafraid of death, as I discussed earlier, is a myth, and this myth is a proof of Japan's having over-extended her war effort. Developing and producing weapons required a great deal of money, you see, but training soldiers did not. It was cheaper to make soldiers willing to be human bombs than to build powerful tanks. We feel good about ourselves as long as self-conceit is maintained, but when reality sets in, the inevitable result is a disaster.

I believe Japanese soldiers on the battlefields were more wretched than their counterparts elsewhere. The price of a soldier is a cent and half, they used to say in those days, as the notice sent to draft a man required a one-and-a-half cent stamp. Summoned by a postcard, mandated to be brave, and treated as cheap, disposable parts, many of these soldiers were killed in the end. Nothing is more horrid. And their wretchedness began during their training. We've heard too many appalling stories of low-ranking officers' cruel and humiliating treatment of new conscripts. I'm sure some officers were cruel by nature, but such treatment was probably necessary to create combat men, capable of killing, out of easy-going sons of farmers who had never seen firearms before. It was not like training men who are used to handling a gun. (Japan and America are of two different military traditions: one had just come out of two hundred and some years of peaceful slumber without even a civil war, and the other was a nation built by killing the native inhabitants of its land.)

Imperial Japan couldn't think of anything else but to produce strong soldiers and a powerful military, and its leaders were impatient and overly eager in this attempt. Top leaders of the military issued numerous orders prohibiting cruel treatment of soldiers, but they had little success. Those who were trained in a ruthless manner would, as they subsequently did, also treat enemy soldiers and civilians ruthlessly. Blame for these incomparable horrors and atrocities, in my mind, goes to career military men who disregarded their soldiers' lives. As shown in Navy terminology, "using a stick to infuse them with spirit," those who practiced cruelty believed, most likely, that such treatment was a necessary process in making strong soldiers. Officers themselves were under enormous pressure caused by their poor country trying to fight against a rich one.

When the war ended with defeat inevitably, Japan went to the other extreme. But, for now, consider some of the statements we hear widely today. For example, that it was war-loving militarists who are responsible for Japan's aggression in the Showa era, or, that the path to the war was taken vis-a-vis earlier Meiji government's policies of making the nation rich and strong. Not considering what had preceded it, this statement does not delineate the history of modern Japan accurately. It does not consider the threat Japan had felt under the military power and pressure displayed by Commodore Perry and European nations, as well as the sense of humiliation and chagrin felt in having to accept the unequal treaties. The statement does not allow a possible interpretation that it was natural and understandable for Japan to concentrate on building a strong military under the circumstances.

Japan converted herself to pacifism after the war and began the task of pleasing the United States eagerly. Deeply affected by defeat, people closed their eyes to the fact of conversion and pretended that the shift to the other end—pacifism—was their own choice. Peace was the absolute good, they now said; nothing else was important and anything that had been related to the war, or promoted the idea of war for that matter, was evil. Having led a life of submission to the rules of groups, as well as to the military dictates, the Japanese now wanted to disregard their past. They believed that acting freely and as they pleased was a way to show their humanity. What we see today in the classrooms of our schools, with destructive students and frequent disturbances, is the result of this philosophy of advocating free expression of desire and will. Bravery, which was regarded with utmost respect during the war, has lost its value and fallen badly.

The recent bus hijacking incident in Saga Prefecture is indicative of this change. The male passengers all fled, either threatened by the hijacker or on their own, leaving the female passengers behind. One woman was killed, with several injured in this incident. If this sort of incident had happened in pre-war times, the male passengers, even though they were scared of a hijacker armed with a knife, probably would have managed to bring the situation under control. If they had run away, forsaking women, they would have been shamed and laughed at as cowards, and the stain of such an unmanly conduct would have lasted for as long as they lived. In order to avoid being called spineless— intolerable for any men in those days—they would have stayed on and fought the hijacker, I would imagine. Things changed after the war, however. People now think only a fool would engage in such a reckless task and risk his life. They may be badly hurt, so it's best not get involved. They rationalize that life is precious and protecting it is the right thing to do, something for which no one could be blamed. In this moral atmosphere, no one would risk themselves by helping women passengers. Typical post-war Japanese pacifists are like those men in the hijacked bus. The pre-war moral concept that "only a coward acts dishonorably" has disappeared; it is obsolete.

This new attitude is no doubt a reaction to the treatment the Japanese endured during the war. It is a rejection of the view, shown in *kamikaze* attacks and other military practices, that life is disposable, trading deaths for national pride. The reaction took them to the other extreme and to abandoning much of their pride. And it is not just men who have lost pride. Consider, for example, young women who are said to gather around the US military bases seeking sex with American soldiers. These women are not trying to sell their bodies to earn money nor to satisfy their own sexual needs, but simply to be able to say that they had sex with an American. These young women are not prostitutes in an ordinary sense, since they are not using their bodies as tools to satisfy and degrade their customers. By letting the servicemen use their bodies, these women seem to be disregarding their sense of pride. It is said that they don't mind being called by such names as "bitches" or "street-girls," but perhaps they don't understand the meaning of those words.

The men who fled from the hijacked bus and the women who seek neither money nor pleasure in return for their sex are both accepting the given without any attempts to oppose or challenge. They risk nothing, and they don't even feel anger. Circumstances then might appear peaceful on the surface, but allowing others to do whatever they please and not countering with resistance seems to reveal a state of mind in which something very important is missing. Japan's pacifists, who refuse to see anything but peace, exhibit a narrow vision and inflexibility, both of which remind me of pre-war militarism and of its readiness to jump at every opportunity to go to war.

Chapter Six

Universality of American Culture

The way the Japanese archipelago is situated is such that one might call it a geographical miracle. On the continent beyond the ocean is China, with an older, dominant civilization. While close enough to be influenced by this Chinese civilization, the Japanese islands are not too close for easy invasion. Accidental, of course, but it is almost too good to be true, making me wonder if there is any other country that has benefited from such an extremely favorable geographical condition. (England, another island country, may be said to be in a similar situation, but, as you know, one can swim across the English Channel; the Strait of Tsushima off Japan is nothing like it.) If the islands were situated quite far from the continental civilization, the inhabitants, like those of the South Pacific, might have been content with their own more relaxed, or "uncivilized," ways. But since the Japanese had seen a glimpse of an advanced civilization, contentment in isolation was not an option. No doubt this geographical advantage has helped shape the characteristics of the people who settled there and influenced the nature of the country they created.

The advantageous location in which the Japanese found themselves was also quite convenient. They were able to pick what they wanted from the neighboring civilizations and when they wanted, to modify them to suit their own needs instead of exerting efforts to create their own. They were also able to shut themselves in and shield themselves from outside influences when they wished to do so.

In the modern era, when more advanced ways to navigate the oceans, as well as to fly the skies were introduced, this advantage ceased to exist. When American Commodore Matthew Perry arrived off Tokyo Bay in 1853, people on the islands of Japan were confronted by this fact for the first time.

Suddenly, Japan found itself in a cutthroat world where its mere survival was tenuous. People understood things had to be done differently. But how? Feeling lost, and suffering from great anxiety, they struggled. First they tried to make Japan like the Western powers, and pushed themselves along the lines of militarism and expansionism. When that failed, they decided to give up autonomy as well as the idea of self-determination. How to find ways to live in this new world devoid of old grace, in fact, has been a major problem for the Japanese in the entire modern era. Acting as if it belongs to the United States, Japan has tried to find its sense of national identity, as well as world recognition in economic achievement and prosperity. But people haven't felt altogether comfortable; they don't know what to do with themselves even today.

Recounting the dreams of the past, some people conclude that Japan's misfortunes began when its door was forced open to the outside world. Living on their islands away from other people is a better way, they would say. But such an option is no longer possible. First of all, what the land produces is not enough to feed today's population of more than120 million. The problem of food shortages might be solved if the population were to be kept at the level of the Tokugawa era (30 million) and the people were to eat modestly. But there are other problems as well. Dreaming will not do. The task the Japanese must tackle now is to find out how to think and conduct themselves in a reality where the world is one big place.

ACCEPTING AMERICAN CULTURE

Japan, you see, has been choosing between isolating and opening herself to the outside, depending on the needs of the time. During the Asuka and Nara period (7th and 8th centuries), it sent envoys to Tang China to learn many things. But then, in the Heian period (794–1185), it suddenly withdrew to its own world and produced a culture centered around its court aristocracy (as embodied in *The Tale of Genji*, reputedly the world's oldest novel). Toward the end of that era, it opened itself up again and traded with China, only to close down once again in the Kamakura period (1185–1333), when Genghis Khan's empire was being formed on the continent just across the ocean.

It was Genghis, not Matthew D. Perry, who first threatened Japan with a powerful military, urging it to open its door. The authority in Kamakura refused to do so and ordered the execution of the envoy who had brought Kublai's message. The Mongolian invasion was repeated during the 13th century, showing how determined Kublai was to take over Japan, and revealing that his intent was to colonize. His soldiers are said to have carried farming equipment with them. The invasion was halted, however, because of the strong winds, *shimpu* or *kamikaze*, which blew favorably for Japan at the crucial moment, destroying the Mongol fleet.

A century or so later, the Sengoku era saw many provincial wars, but the door to Japan was kept open without any forcing or urging. Political leaders in this time experienced the culture of the Europeans, who were called "Southern Barbarians." Oda Nobunaga, a major provincial lord who took control of much of the land for a brief period, is said to have enjoyed good wine as well as other Western things; he also let seminaries be built and allowed Christian missionaries to do their work in Japan. Later, as rumors spread that missionaries were cheating farmers in order to sell them away as slaves (it was also feared that Spain, after having colonized the Philippines, had an eye on Japan for invasion), Christianity was deemed dangerous. Successive rulers also got tired of the culture of "Southern Barbarians." So the door was closed once again. During the era of the Tokugawa shogunate (1603–1867), total closure of the country (except for Holland, China and Korea) became the strict policy. Indigenous culture, such as *kabuki* theater, flourished, and peace and stability were maintained for over two hundreds years.

At the very end of the Tokugawa period, when the Japanese were confronted with outside forces once again, they found that this time they were in an entirely new situation—they had no choice. Unlike previous occasions, this time an opening was forced, and it was in a humiliating manner without a possibility of shutting the door.

To think about it, Japan's repeated movement of opening up and closing down to the outside world is symptomatic of a psychological state in which the inner self is separated from the outer self. Whether it is with free will or by force, opening a country to the outside world means letting foreign cultures come in and influence the indigenous people. Anyhow, after her defeat in the Pacific War Japan was placed, as she was in the last years of the Tokugawa period, under powerful outside influences—this time, American.

Perhaps because of their tendency toward self-centeredness, most Americans seem to think their culture is entirely legitimate, even superior, while the Japanese is inferior, missing something important (I see this in Ruth Benedict's *The Chrysanthemum and the Sword*, which, I am aware, was written by the request of the US government to aid American understanding of Japanese culture). Not totally consciously and without malicious intent, the Americans tried to make the Japanese become like them. Perhaps wanting to turn Japan into a Christian country, and, thinking they could, they poured in a great deal of money and effort. Making sure that Japan would not become an enemy for the United States again was another goal, of course.

I am of the generation which remembers having felt uncomfortable with many things that had landed with the American cultural invasion. Men in the US military chewed gum while walking, for instance. Having been taught that only badly mannered people would keep food in their mouth while walking, the sight came across to me as distasteful. Japanese who were born after the war do not share this sentiment, I am sure, because I often see them eating candies on the train and walking with hamburgers in their hand. (There is nothing wrong with it because no one suffers from it, these people would say, and I cannot argue with them. Still, having received a pre-war education, I feel uncomfortable. I cannot help it and these things are difficult to change.) Kissing in public is another example of American influence. Once, kissing was explicitly a sexual act in Japan. Although we have eventually gotten used to "pan-pan girls" (as street prostitutes for US servicemen were called) kissing their customers on the street, it was shocking for most Japanese, who must have felt they witnessed the first step of sex in public. Pre-war Japanese movies showed no kiss scenes, and even in those made immediately after the war, kisses were only implied by shifting the camera from faces to the lower part of bodies (clothed, of course) and by showing the woman's heel moving slightly upward.

I wonder if a freer expression of love and affection, particularly in public places, is also an American influence. Some may argue that the Japanese were once quite open in expressing love and that they have merely gone back to that old custom. But in the modern era, the Japanese were uptight in mixing genders, and the attitude enforced at schools was "after age seven boys and girls are not to sit together." Merely walking on the street with a girl was a target of teasing then, and married couples followed the doctrine of "three steps behind," with the wife walking a bit behind the husband. People cannot fathom these practices today, and it is good that those silly customs died out. Although I find walking with food in the mouth unsightly, it is nice to see a man and a woman walking hand in hand.

Japan's traditional practices and social mores, as well as aesthetics, were not all good and wonderful. Some in fact were ridiculous. So, by accepting American freedom and democracy, the Japanese gained many good things. Particularly welcome to me was that we no longer had to follow the mandate of "obeying your parents and teachers." I can now say "No" to what I don't want to do, I remember having said to myself. In short, American influences on the Japanese life style in the postwar era were both enforced and freely chosen. To say that everything was the result of a cultural invasion backed up by military power is incorrect and counterproductive. Japanese people were not forced to eat walking, or to walk hand-in-hand.

CULTURAL UNIVERSALITY AND SPECIFICITY

When we look at two cultures, American and Japanese, it is clear that the latter has been more heavily influenced by the former. The Japanese are definitely Americanized, while the presence of Japanese culture in America is quite limited—to sushi, karaoke, and a few other things. But this imbalance is not necessarily due to an enforcement that went hand-in-hand with the US military occupation. I believe that all cultures are different, that each has its own specificity and uniqueness. There isn't such a thing as universal culture. Although no culture is universal, the degree of universality or non-universality differs from culture to culture, however. Some are, relatively speaking, more universal than others: American and Japanese cultures are different in the degree of universality.

Japanese culture has been created and fostered by people who lived on islands situated in a rare geographical location, and for some reason they have shared an illusion that they were all tied together by blood (even though they were actually of many different origins). And these people had a luxury of relating to the outsider only when they wanted to do so. Theirs is a culture conceived and nurtured to be shared only among themselves. On the other hand, American culture has been shaped by many different elements, just as the country is made up of all kinds of people. There are WASPs, of course, but before them were Native Americans. Then, Europeans of various regional origins joined, along with Africans brought in as slaves, as well as the Hispanics. Since the country's population is a mixture of many different types of people, American culture is something like the highest common denominator.

America is a country of people who, with their many different backgrounds, live and work together to arrive at the point where agreements are achieved, more or less. Their history has biases, rationalizations and concealment, and since the country is made up of people who don't share a common root and tradition, mutual mistrust is naturally deep and prevalent. On points where the Japanese can reach mutual understanding with relative ease, Americans go to court to settle. They have to go through many processes, which to the outsider appear unnecessary.

If a person who is neither American nor Japanese were to live somewhere other than their own native land, it would be easier for him(her) to adjust to American culture than to Japanese. American culture can be understood and accepted by a greater number of people. In other words, it has greater universality. No one can deny this. In the United States, for example, anyone, even a newcomer, can contest a dispute so long as they have the money to hire a lawyer. In Japan, on the other hand, the same newcomer, who will be seen as an outsider, would be lost. Japan is like a village where people conduct their business under unspoken rules. Disputes are solved according to rules about which no one is very clear.

There is also a big difference between Japan and America in the way that non-natives are accepted. I often hear complaints made by foreigners living in Japan. Having lived for a long time in Japan, or even being naturalized, they say they are still treated as *gaijin*, an outer person. If they have an excellent command of the language, moreover, they are seen with a certain suspicion. Holding onto a belief, single-mindedly, that Japanese culture cannot be understood by foreigners, the Japanese are narrow-minded, indeed. Americans, on the other hand, are much more open-minded to the newcomer. Except for Native Americans, they were all outsiders once, after all, and although you hear about racial prejudice a great deal, most Americans seem to think such prejudice is unacceptable. Contrary to this, the Japanese take it for granted that it is all right to exclude outsiders, white or black, and they probably don't see such exclusion as racial prejudice.

The two cultures are not equal in this sense. American culture surpasses that of Japan in the degree with which it is accepted by other people with ease, and in the capacity with which it accepts other cultures. Take a look at Japanese universities and research institutions, for example, where talented individuals tend to be ostracized so that an orderly sense of seniority, as well as harmony, among all concerned can be maintained. By trying not to subject yourself to such an ostracism, you might end up sacrificing your talent in such places. It is better to go to the United States, some conclude, and such individuals are not rare.

It is true that Americans do a better job in many areas, but that does not mean their culture is superior. Japanese and American cultures are simply of a different kind. We know that books that sell well are not necessarily of a higher quality. They may sell well simply because they cater to a more popular taste. The reverse is not necessarily true, of course, and there are also books that don't sell because they are uninteresting and of little value. In any event, one cannot say that a culture with greater universality is more valuable. Still, that American culture surpasses Japanese culture in terms of universality and accessibility is unrefutable.

Be it Japanese, Chinese or African, for example, people in general find Western clothing better when they want to be active. In fact it is difficult to relax in a Japanese kimono or traditional hairdo. Because they are more convenient and easier to wear, Western clothes are now the choice of more people, and this fact has contributed to make an aspect of Western culture dominant—the winner, if you will. One might speculate, then, that convenience and ease have something to do with cultural universality. Until the end of World War Two, most women wore kimonos in Japan and Western clothes were worn only by men when they went to work. After a while, men stopped wearing the kimono altogether and women, too, came to wear it only on special occasions, such as graduations or weddings. Today, the kimono has given way to Western clothing entirely. That is what has happened. The shift is totally understandable, and is nothing one should complain or argue about.

The presence of fast food chains such as Kentucky Fried Chicken and Mac-Donald's is quite conspicuous in Japan today, having spread all over the country. Since the same phenomenon has been observed elsewhere, say in France, the invasion of fast food chains is not the result of the American victory over Japan in the last war. Since sushi bars and restaurants serving tempura and teriyaki are found in great numbers in the United States, food culture has probably nothing to do with the outcome of the war. Think of Chinese food, which seems to have conquered the world, with restaurants in all its corners.

What about advertisements? According to a friend who has researched television commercials, Japanese advertising agencies use Caucasian models quite frequently (68.1% in clothing advertising, but also in cigarettes, whiskey, soft drinks, cars and cosmetics—Kozakai Toshiaki, *Les Japonais sont-ills des Occidentaux?*, 1991). I was surprised at this finding because the phenomenon of Caucasians advertising in a non-Caucasian country seems a bit odd. It may be the case, however, that products advertised by a person representing the winner nation have more authority, or so advertising firms think.

While I see little influence of the war in Japanese food consumption, the story is different in the area of their sexual behavior. I often hear of Japanese men who seem to have a strong interest in sleeping with a Caucasian women. According to a tour guide friend of mine, his Japanese male clients start talking about sleeping with French prostitutes the minute they set foot in Paris. Also, Caucasian prostitutes in Tokyo are said to be able to command much higher prices than their Japanese counterparts. This may be due to a rarity value perhaps, but it may not be, as in European countries, where, it is said, prostitutes charge pretty much the same regardless of their racial background. And what about those young Japanese women who were called "yellow cabs"? This is a reference to New York cabs, but "yellow" also connotes the color of the skin; while taxies would pick up anyone who hailed for a fee, these women, they say, are free. I have already mentioned young Japanese women who for some reason want to sleep with American servicemen. In the matter of sexual behavior like this, I cannot but suspect a psychology of the defeated. I sense an inferiority complex that seeks to be sexually united with the conqueror, to compensate, perhaps. Since I happen to hold a theory that our sexual behavior is based on our illusions, I can understand the minds of these Japanese men and women. If their sexual interest is based on their need to compensate, however, they could end up with more inferiority, not less.

Chapter Seven

Reconsidering *Wa,* Harmony

Japan today is open to the outside world, unlike in the era of the shoguns, and so, some argue, foreigners who want to come to live and work in Japan should be given a chance to do so. Others oppose this position, dividing the nation, and the issue is not easy to sort out. No one can deny that Japan's economy depends a great deal on its import and export industries. The country in fact is only thirty percent self-sufficient in food supply, and this means that if the importing of food were to stop, the majority of Japanese would starve. We also know that the Japanese can afford their affluent lifestyle because they can sell products overseas. The argument that it is selfish of Japan to be unwilling to let foreign workers come in, while earning a great deal in export businesses, is right on track.

It seems to me, however, the Japanese in general still entertain a desire to isolate themselves. They yearn for the time when they were isolated. This state of mind is probably related to the trauma Japan experienced earlier, of having been dragged out of their long hibernation. The popularity of the recent NHK (Japan Broadcasting) drama series, *Oedo de gozaru* ("It's in Edo We Are") may have something to do with the nostalgia held by the Japanese for the time when there were no foreigners about. If I allow myself to repeat my analogy of the forced opening of the country to that of a rape, the woman, having experienced sexual violation, continues to have negative feelings toward intercourse no matter how much reasoning she applies to convince herself that sex is enjoyable.

ACCEPTING FOREIGNERS

In one of his controversial speeches, Ishihara Shintaro, the Governor of Tokyo, cautioned against foreigners illegally residing in Japan's many cities, and whose increased numbers might be contributing to the rising rate of crime (although I wonder if it is really true that "picking" break-ins, with a special tool to break locks, are mostly committed by illegal Chinese residents). The speech has caused some controversy, and although some social critics and commentators criticized Ishihara, many Tokyorites applauded. This, I think, is a sign of what may be called a xenophobic mood. Since the Japanese have a history of mass paranoia, and once accused and persecuted Korean residents for allegedly tampering with neighborhood wellss, using poison, in the aftermath of the Great Kanto Earthquake (in 1922), their anti-foreigner sentiments must be carefully examined. Are the crimes committed by foreigners actually increasing? Is the rate of their crimes higher than that of those committed by the Japanese? Are foreigners likely to commit more serious crimes? Particular types of crimes? We have to answer these questions first instead of jumping to conclusions. The situation has to be examined objectively to see if we are not swayed merely by a mood.

It is true crimes seem more horrible when committed by foreigners. In general, such crimes make people more anxious about rules and the safety of their daily lives. It may also be true that foreigners are more difficult to apprehend. Crimes are a cultural phenomenon, and how they are committed and how they are solved differ in each culture and society. Certain types of crime are not likely to be committed by the Japanese, which, however, does not mean that the Japanese have a higher morality. The rate of serious crimes, such as murder and rape, is considerably lower in Japan than in the United States or other industrialized countries, and Japanese police officials seem to take this as a sign of their excellence. But as various incidents in more recent years have shown, Japanese police are neither that excellent nor very capable. Naturally, preventing unfamiliar kinds of crimes is harder, and Japanese police are not good at dealing with the type of crimes rarely committed by the Japanese. Can they successfully combat the types of crimes more likely to be committed by foreigners? Some people are asking and they worry about possible problems that might arise by allowing foreigners to come in freely.

I suspect the real reason for Japan's excellent crime statistics lies elsewhere. Japanese criminals, like the rest of the Japanese, tend to give in easily to authority. Being timid or overly serious, they confess with little pressure. A popular television drama series, *Mito Komon*, is a good example to show what the common Japanese attitude toward authority is like. The drama is about the adventures of a revered former senior adviser to the Tokugawa shogunate, now in disguise. Each episode ends with a scene where a small emblem is shown confronting the bad guys at the crucial moment. Since the emblem reveals the identity of the revered Komon, the corrupt samurai surrenders on the spot. This ending is not entirely nonsensical in the mind of

viewers, who seem to enjoy the drama without much questioning of its validity. It points to a collective illusion held by the Japanese: bad guys would
not challenge authority.

Where else but in Japan do we find bad guys so docile, so submissive? Neither in America nor in Russia, certainly. Their criminals do not so readily give
in, and if a drama with a scene similar to the ending of *Mito Komon* were to
be aired there, their audience would take it as a comedy, if not a bizarre joke.
Although I am not saying that Japanese criminals are all like those in this
drama series, there are more of them in Japan than in Russia or in America,
making it possible to conclude that the Japanese police are not well prepared
for tougher criminals as well as umfamiliar ones. As I said earlier, human beings are animals with their instincts no longer intact, and to keep society in
order, some kind of artificial measures have to be enforced. How that enforcement is carried out differs from society to society; so does how the criminals break and resist the enforcement. The way Japanese society enforces order is different from the ways it is done in other societies, and in this sense
Japanese culture, while it is neither better nor worse, is different from others.

What is in sharp contrast with that of Japan is a monotheistic culture with
one absolute God, a culture that has laws given by that God. Social order is
maintained by religious teachings and by the enforcement of clearly and
straightforwardly written laws. Although Japanese society certainly has
norms and rules that regulate people's behavior, laws and teachings are not so
clearly laid out. Doing so has never been very important to the Japanese because of the geographical and historical peculiarities they had enjoyed (to
which I have referred earlier). Thus, the Japanese tend to do without verbal-
ization unless the need is urgent. It is a difficult undertaking for them. It is extremely difficult to talk about mores and rules existing in Japanese society,
but I will try my best to explain.

JAPANESE VIEWS ON HUMAN NATURE

Norms dictating many aspects of Japanese culture hold a particular view re-
garding human nature, and this view is rarely expressed in words. Most
Japanese are not even aware of it, at least most of the time. They adhere to
this view of human nature, however, believing it to be universal. I would not
go so far as to say that this view is "unique," but the Japanese characteristi-
cally think that not only they but the rest of the world also subscribes to it. If
not, they think, it should. This theory, of course, is based on some kind of illusion, and therefore, the question we should ask is why the Japanese have
come to entertain such an illusion.

"There's no ogre in this world where we live" is an old Japanese saying that summarizes this view. It can be explained as follows. Human beings are good-tempered by nature, and while gentle and well-meaning, they are not very strong, and are easily harmed. So much so that the only way they can survive is through mutual support. People may resort to wrongdoing in extenuating circumstances, or they may be temporarily out of touch with themselves and lose their good judgment. Even criminals, however, have a soft spot somewhere in their heart, and so long as they are allowed to restore it, they will regain their good self and regret what they have done. When they repent, it is best to forgive them rather than persecute. True, some are truly wicked, but they are exceptions; they are closer to monsters or beasts than humans.

Dramas and stories that have enjoyed wide appeal over many years in Japan are almost always based on this view of human nature. Although individual members may not be always conscious of the fact, societal norms and orders are constructed around this view. In fact, it has a direct link to the ways people relate to each other. Based on their premise that human beings are weak and easily hurt, and not placing high values on independence and the self-assertion of the individual, the Japanese concentrate on finding out how others are feeling, and they expect others to do the same (this is a form of *amae*). The notion that people are good by nature also leads the Japanese to believe that trust is of utmost importance.

Judging from their belief that social order can be maintained through sincerity and truthfulness, some may conclude that all Japanese must be good and gentle. This is not so. Japanese history is full of conflicts and troubles, particularly with neighboring countries. The problem, I believe, lies in the unexamined assumption held by the Japanese that others share the same view of human nature. When they find out that this is not the case, and others don't act as expected, they become disappointed, even feeling betrayed. And, of course they are bound to be disappointed.

The view of human nature commonly held by the Japanese is not realistic. It is biased, and it does not accurately reflect people in the real world. As to whether human beings are fundamentally good or not, various sages have endlessly argued in many cultures without the definitive answer to this day. But in our daily lives, we see ample examples that go against the common Japanese view of human nature. People do not commit crimes only under unfortunate circumstances. There are times when the most sincere apology is not accepted. Some people never repent their wrongdoing, and there are those who would take advantage of others whenever they can.

I often hear about the complaints many Japanese have in meeting and dealing with foreigners. They feel strained, and it is exhausting, they say. Such an experience is stressful because the Japanese hold a particular view of human nature. When they live in foreign countries, the Japanese tend to form a community of their own, sticking together among themselves, not mixing with other people. Most Japanese also prefer to take sightseeing trips abroad in a group, and they don't attempt to make personal connections with the people of the land they visit, coming back only with their shopping experiences. This is not necessarily because of language difficulty, but because it is easier and more comfortable to deal only with fellow Japanese. It is best, they think, to avoid possible discomfort to start with.

Another example of Japanese reluctance in dealing with foreigners can be found in the presence of trading companies, which are collectively called *shosha* (examples are Mitsubishi Shoji and Mitsui Bussan). *Shosha*, I think, is a uniquely Japanese institution. When American or European companies and manufacturers try to sell their products, they do so without an intermediary firm who exclusively engages in overseas sales. But in Japan, it is the *shosha,* with its specially trained staffs, that takes on this job. Ordinary companies and manufacturers are considered unfit in negotiating with foreigners, and although the number of *shosha* has decreased in more recent years, Japanese companies have needed them as dealers with foreigners.

Communicating with foreigners and establishing personal relationships is difficult, particularly if we insist on holding onto our own particular views of human nature. Because they believe them to be the foundation of an orderly world, however, the Japanese cannot discard their views on human nature. If they did, the world, they think, would be destroyed. This is one of the main reasons why the Japanese who visit abroad or live there tend to stay together, shutting themselves into their own world and taking it for granted.

The concept of *wa*, or harmony, is also deeply rooted in the Japanese view on human nature. A prevailing attitude among the Japanese is that forgiveness should be granted without reparation if the person repents and apologizes with utmost sincerity. This attitude has the idea of *wa* as its basis. (which, by the way, may have caused friction between Japan and some Asian countries on the issue of war crimes.) In old times, the most serious apology was given in the act of disembowelment—*hara-kiri* or *seppuku.* In such expressions as "black bellied" and "read the belly," the Japanese seem to have located the core of being in the lower abdomen. *Seppuku,* therefore, is to cut the abdomen open in order to show their core, to reveal the truth about themselves. People even now strongly believe *wa* is essential in good relationships, and the state of *wa* can be achieved by being considerate of each other and not putting one's need first.

CURTAILING OF MIND

The main deterrent for a Japanese against wrongdoing is the fear of being criticized or rejected by *seken*. *Seken* is an entity which consists of people to whom one has to relate beyond one's immediate family. In his novel, *Kusamakura (Three-Cornered World)*, Natsume Soseki says the following:

"This world is created neither by god nor goblins but by the ordinary people who are around us, those who live opposite and next door; even if you don't like to be in this world, where else can you go? It'll have to be the world of "non-human" and that place will be even more difficult to live in."

By "this worled,"*hito no yo*, Soseki means not the Western world with almighty God as well as demons, but *seken*. The Japanese perception of "this world" is a place where there is no God; a place, therefore, without a divine order. Exclusion from *seken* means there is no other place to go. It is only natural for the Japanese to pay close attention to the eye of the people around them.

Although the word *wa*, harmony, does connote a blissful state full of good will and free of conflict, it has a negative side to it as well. As is always the case, there are a few outsiders who are sacrificed in the name of harmony for a group or a community. Take, for example, the case of hemophiliac patients, about whom we've heard so much in recent years. Their tragedy (of contracting AIDS via transfusion) was caused by individuals who had promoted *wa* among their groups—bureaucrats of the Ministry of Health and Welfare, the pharmaceutical company who hired retired Ministry officials as advisors, and the physicians receiving funds for their research from the pharmaceutical company. Left outside of this *wa* circle are the hemophiliac patients who died as sacrificial lambs.

Bullying a person who has done nothing wrong, but disruptws *wa*, is also a problematic trait of Japanese communities. An old saying, "a stake that sticks out will be beaten down," means that a person with an exceptional talent is fated to have that talent stifled because he has disturbed*wa*. by inviting jealousy among other members of the group. The group that denies, even tries to get rid of an individual with special talent, does so because it can afford to. In the world of fierce competition, a talented individual will be chosen as the leader. The group will support and make use of such a talent because otherwise it will lose in the competition and be obliterated. In other words, it will not be able to afford a mood such as *wa*.

Judging from such old sayings as the one on the stake that sticks out, Japan in its pre-modern era must have been a place where maintaining *wa* harmony was crucially important. The country has since been dragged into a highly competitive world where *wa* is a luxury it can hardly afford. People continue to hold onto it, however, out of habit. Even the military, engaging in the matter of life and death, considered it important, and when they were in disagreement on strategy development, leaders opted to listening to both sides, trying to find a compromise. Because they as a group were so eager to maintain *wa* among themselves, decisions to keep incompetent commanders and staff officers were made, just to save their face.

The peculiar view of human nature the Japanese seem to share could cause problems in the individual psyche as well as in interpersonal and international relationships. Although most Japanese have some elements and tendencies that go against this view within themselves, they tend to repress them, and the result is a distorted self-image and a warp, as it were, in their personality structure. Even if repression doesn't take place, they most likely try to hide those elements from other people, making them virtually hypocrites. Many Japanese do not find it easy to accept realities that go against their views of human nature. Whenever it is difficult to do so, they tend to categorize the problematic situation as "cause unknown," resulting in no measures to prevent it from happening again. Some mistakes are thus repeated again and again, but as the fact that mistakes were made is denied, victims are left as they are and reasons for mistakes go unexamined. This is why, in part, the Japanese get in trouble both internationally and among themselves.

Misunderstandings happen all the time, but as the causes are hidden, problems are not cleared up. I am not arguing here whether this view is good or bad, but by holding an inflexible and unrealistic view of human nature, and by believing it to be universal without carefully examining and discussing it, the Japanese people invite unexpected and uncalled-for problems.

Conflict resolution is often difficult for the Japanese because they are not used to open discussions and verbal disputation as a means to deal with conflicts. As a consequence, they tend to either give in and internalize their dissatisfaction (if the opponent is powerful), or push their way without sufficient explanations (in dealing with the weaker). An individual who is deemed an "outsider," one who doesn't share the view mentioned above, is doomed in Japan. Since clear rules and standards are not given, such an individual is usually unaware of mistakes he(she) has made. There is no chance to protest (what to protest one often does not know), and the outcome is discrimination and ostracism.

I have listed all the negative attributes of the *wa* spirit, but there are also positive features, one of which is the likelihood of avoiding violent confrontations. Unlike in a monotheistic culture, where opposing factions insist on their views vehemently, proponents of *wa* are always ready to compromise. Although exact figures are not available, the death toll of all civil wars ever fought in Japan from the twelfth to the nineteenth century was far smaller than in Europe. The French Revolution and Meiji Restoration both brought social changes of a similar scope, but while the number of French killed by their own people (not including those who died in the battles fought against other countries) was about 600,000; those killed in the struggle that led to the Meiji Restoration is said to have been less than 10,000 (an additional 20,000 if casualties in the Seinan War, which was fought after the new government was elected, are included). People who value their principles do not yield easily; they would go after those they deem their enemies, and they are as thorough as they can be, resorting, in the worst case, to killing them off. Advocates of *wa*, on the other hand, are easy, even sloppy, on principles, and they don't mind compromising. This, of course, does not seem to apply in modern warfare, where the Japanese were ever more ready to kill.

Just as we cannot say that the traditional Japanese view is all negative, we would not want to say that the view of human nature fostered in monotheistic cultures is better. I would say, however, that the Japanese reluctance to spell out their view clearly and objectively is a fatal shortcoming. The days when they lived on islands among themselves have long gone. In this age, when there is no choice but to relate to the people with whom they don't share the same basic views and premises, it is crucially important to have the standards and premises that they live by clearly stated. How just and perfect these standard are does not matter so much, but they must be spelled out, ready for discussion.

Japan could not close its door to the outside world again, even if it wanted to. It is imperative for the Japanese, therefore, to begin verbalizing their views of human nature, which they have long kept as an unspoken truth. Only then will they be able to make these views clear in their conscious minds and be able to examine them in a broader perspective. Otherwise, the Japanese will end up being the world's most maladjusted people.

Chapter Eight

The Tokyo Tribunal and America's Illness

Puraido: unmei no shunkan ("The Pride: A Fatal Moment," directed by Itoh Shunnya, released in 1998) is a movie about the Far East War Criminal Tribunals with Tōjō Hideki as the main character. Its opening scene depicts Tōjō at home, trying to commit suicide before imminent arrest by military police of the occupational government. His failure to do so caused a great deal of damage to his reputation. Since there were more than a few—Minister of the Army Anami Koreiku and Lieutenant-General Ohnishi Takijirō among them—who had already committed *seppuku*, disembowelment following the prescribed protocol, Tōjō's survival was met with scorn by the general public. He was considered a coward and unfit to be a career military man.

A person's worth should be determined, I think, by what one accomplishes while alive, but according to Japanese tradition, you see, it has been by the way one dies; an aesthetic of dying, you might call it. In any event, people made Tōjō a laughing stock, saying that he failed because his hand shook, because he was afraid, and so on. In the years immediately after the end of the war, career military men in general were made into villains, and Tōjō, being both head of the military and also prime minister at the time when Japan went to war, was a scapegoat. The public, which had suffered from a major loss in self-esteem, took his failure at suicide as being superimposed on the nation's losses and mistakes, for which the military was held responsible. The occupational government, controlling the Japanese media, might have encouraged this view.

Whether Tōjō really deserved such bad treatment is a matter one needs to carefully examine, since there are many questions about him that haven't been fully answered. The movie "The Pride" seems to try to do this task by presenting him not so much as an individual but as one who embodied general thoughts of the time. It presents a view that tries to defend Japan of that time by defending Tōjō's position.

A METHOD SUBTLE YET PENETRATING

There are some aspects of the movie with which I agree and some with which I disagree. The part I don't agree with is its depiction of the Greater East Asian War, with an overly sympathetic interpretation of Japan's position. I hold an opinion that the war was not entirely an aggressive invasion and that Japan had both legitimate points to make and the issues to be heard. But the movie tells the story in such a way that it makes Japan look as if she fought the war in order to rescue Asia from Western colonialism. I don't believe that was the case.

It is true there was such an aspect, and in fact countries under the colonial rules of Britain, America, France and Holland at the beginning of the war have since achieved independence. Although to say that Japan went to war to help the countries gain their independence is entirely inaccurate, there were soldiers who believed in the idea of liberating Asia. A troop stationed in Indonesia, for example, provided the native independence fighters with weapons without the order of their commanders and disregarding the Allied Forces' order not to do so (the troop used the pretext that they had merely discarded weapons that were not functioning). Also, about 2,000 Japanese soldiers are said to have died fighting against Dutch troops, which had returned to regain their colony.

If you want to insist that Japan's goal was to free Asia from Western colonizers, however, you have to show exactly what plans the Japanese military had, and how the war was actually fought to reach that goal. Actions of individual soldiers aren't sufficient as the evidence. Furthermore, the Japanese military did not give independence to the people of the lands it occupied (when it did, it was only nominally), and just as the British, French, American and Dutch did, the Japanese exploited native resources and labor forces (a Japanese word *romusha*, laborer, I understand, was used even after the war). Some people have argued that exploitation wasn't Japan's intention, that Indonesian oil and other natural resources were necessary to pursue the war and liberate Asia, and that Asian independence would have been achieved if Japan had won. These words are not convincing at all. Only what was actually done matters in the end.

Although the Japanese military didn't make the liberation of Asia a goal, and although it didn't do anything specific to achieve it, Japanese soldiers did fight against the white people in various parts of Asia, sometimes winning and treating their prisoners of war in deliberately humiliating ways. By seeing the white people to surrender, or act subserviently as if they were afraid of the Japanese, the non-whites of colonized Asia were able to free themselves from an illusion to which they had been bound. They realized that if they fought hard, they might be able to defeat the white race. The white race, you see, was able to colonize Asia and keep it under control for an extended period because it successfully implanted an illusion that the Asians were not its equals, therefore rebellion was futile. (I believe the dynamics between the ruler and the ruled exist more in the realm of illusion than in reality.) The Japanese military broke this mind-set about white superiority, helping the colonized people to lead themselves to liberation on their own. I believe what motivated the military was, primarily, to compensate for their own inferiority complex toward the white race and not to help fellow Asians, however. I suspect British and Dutch former POWs nursed a strong hatred against Japan for so long partially because they were humiliated in front of the people they had previously held in low esteem.

Some kind of connection between the campaigns the Japanese military carried out and Indian independence could be found if we try and force ourselves. And it goes like this: during the Imphale Campaign of 1944 (Japan's advance from Burma to India), Indian soldiers, who had been fighting along with the British and captured in Singapore and the Malay Peninsula, were organized by Chandler Boos to fight for Indian independence, and these soldiers now joined the Japanese campaign. Now, since Boos and his men did fight for India's independence, one cannot totally deny that Japan's Imphale Campaign was fought, in part, for Indian independence as well—but only in part. Japanese troops didn't advance into India to help win Indian independence.

The Imphale Campaign is well-known among the Japanese as a reckless campaign carried out without regard for supply shipments. It naturally ended in total failure, and out of 100,000 soldiers, only 20,000 survived; most of the 80,000 who didn't come back are said to have died of hunger and illnesses. The British government, which wanted to keep India colonized, attempted to have the soldiers who had joined the Imphale Campaign tried for treason. To this, the Indian public stood up, objecting to such a trial. They were angered by the idea of punishing people who had fought for their independence. Facing such large-scale protests, the British colonial government gave in, and that was the beginning of the end of its colonial rule in India. The reason is as follows: the British had ruled India not only militarily but with the power of logic as well; they had held the position, to their credit (and to show their ingenuity) that the Indians were subjects of the British Empire, a premise that rationalized their rule. They therefore had to conduct a treason trial against Indians who had joined in Japan's Imphale Campaign. And it was not possible to carry the trial; this meant that the premise, previously held, was no longer valid, thus the end of British rule based on the power of logic.

British rule over India ended not because the British military lost in a war against Indians, but because rationalization of the rule failed. One can go so far as to say that the Japanese military contributed to the first step, but to claim thatJapan freed India from Britain's rule is simply illogical. Japanese troops didn't advance into India, defeat the British, and leave, letting the people of India do the rest of the work; Japanese contributions to Indian independence were even less than in the case of Indonesia.

In any event, it is wrong to distort facts, as the movie "Pride" does, and imply that Japan fought the war for Asian liberation and that Japan's advance into India helped its independence movement. Even if some connection between the two is to be found, the logic given in the movie is close to nonsensical. One might say that the Greater East Asian War did trigger the liberation of Asian countries, but it did nothing more. As stated in the Imperial Mandate, Japan went to war in self-defense, not to bring justice to Asian neighbors. I don't think a nation starts a war solely to bring justice, although justice has been repeatedly used as an excuse. For example, the Civil War in America was supposedly to abolish slavery, and the Vietnam War (as well as the recent Iraqi war) was to protect freedom and democracy. It was not just Americans who rationalized their wars. The Japanese military's having employed a similar rationalization is not exceptional.

TRIAL BY THE WINNER

The part I can agree with in the movie "Pride" is when it presents the Tokyo War Tribunal as not being properly carried out. Dominated by representatives of the United States, the Tribunal was clearly one-sided. Having the winner of the war rather than an impartial third party judge the defeated was also morally questionable. Furthermore, the Tribunal was based on a rather simplistic premise—the winner takes all, and, following this premise, it decreed that the United States was entirely just and Japan was the aggressor with an inhumane heart. Now, it is one thing to hold such a view, but it is another to base an actual trial on it; it goes against the principle of fairness. Because Americans are known for their strong belief in fairness, I've been puzzled over these years by the way the Tribunal was carried out. In any event, the Tokyo War Tribunal lacked the fairness essential to any trial; it was not a trial, but retribution in the name of trial.

The Japanese, however, accepted the premise on which the trial stood; the premise later came to be referred to as "A View According to the Tokyo War

Tribunal." Japanese postwar education, understanding of democracy, and perception of the US-Japan relationship are all affected by this view. It was in fact the starting point of Japan as we know the nation today.

Now, something is wrong with this view, and anyone who's had a chance to closely examine it will have to agree. Some doubts about it, in fact, have always been in the corner of Japanese minds, smothering them. But no one was able to openly voice them. Since Japan as a nation was defined by it, as it were, rejecting this view meant denying the very existence of the country. When we are not allowed to voice our doubts for a long time, you see, we will eventually convince ourselves into thinking what is wrong to be right. This is because asking questions without receiving any answer keeps us in constant tension, a state most of us cannot sustain for long; it is our human weakness. The Japanese people, therefore, lived post-war years accepting the view demonstrated in the Tokyo War Tribunal as a matter of fact. Some didn't do so easily, however. The movie *Puraido* is an expression of smothered doubts staying in the minds of people.

But why did the United States not only come up with such an obviously unfair notion that the winner can pass judgments on the defeated, but actually went ahead to do so? History, of course, has seen many examples of destroying the enemy with cruelties and enslavement, such as Rome over Carthage, or cases where the conquered were allowed to survive but forced into a burden of heavy reparations, as in the case of post-World War I Germany. In Japanese history during the civil war era (1467–1584), too, the lands of defeated lords were confiscated and the heads of chief warriors were taken as trophies. But never in the entire history of Japan, except in the Tokyo War Tribunal, was an occasion when the winner tried the defeated in the name of justice, deeming the defeated as morally bad. And that was what the United States did. The United States, of course, had a right to occupy Japan as the winner of the war. Toward the end of the war also, many Japanese suspected certain cruel treatment. "Men will all become slaves, while women will be raped," I remember adults around me were saying. While suspected cruelties were not carried out, they soon found out they had to face a kind of cruelty they had not imagined. It had never occurred to them that they were going to be tried for their moral wrongdoing.

It is true that the Japanese military, as well as some individual soldiers, had committed many atrocities. Still, what was the basis for the United States to try these people? The right to be the plaintiff in the trial, in fact, should have been given to the nations and the people of Asia, since most atrocities were carried out in Asia. Or a third party should have been the judge. The Tribunal then would have been more logical and its outcomes easier for the Japanese to accept. For that matter, the Japanese people themselves might have tried their military leaders for their crimes of having led the nation astray and caus-ing a great deal of pain and suffering: something like a people's court. And that would have been also logical.

Atrocities Japan perpetrated against Americans were in the end far less than those the United States perpetrated against the Japanese. If there were to be a logic that the victim can also try the victimizer, can Japan try America for all the things it did, such as murdering surrendered soldiers, killing mas-sive numbers of civilians in air raids, and dropping atomic bombs? That would have been fairer. If the United States' position was to punish certain Japanese military leaders and make them pay with their lives because it was their men who had killed American soldiers, it would be understandable. Not acceptable, but understood as an angry emotional reaction. Japan, even de-feated, did not have to give the United States the right to try it on the basis of justice, however. It should have protested.

There have been other countries besides the United States who have tried en-emy individuals for specific war crimes they committed and given them death sentences. But those countries, I think, would not have thought of passing a judg-ment on defeated nations as a whole, of putting their leaders on trial. This idea is uniquely American. Let's suppose for now that the outcome of the war were different. Turn it around and suppose Japan did what the United States did, in-cluding dropping A-bombs. Imagine, in other words, an entire reversal of his-tory. Would the Japanese have wanted to put the Unites States on trial? There are many different types of people among the Japanese, but at least I wouldn't be part of such a trial; it would make me feel ashamed of myself. Although our en-emy was atrocious, I would reason if I were an American, we also dropped A-bombs and performed other criminal acts. I don't want to blame only the enemy because doing so would inevitably invite some self-doubt in the mind. If there were any occasion when Japan judged a defeated enemy nation as corrupt, and sentenced its leaders to death as criminals, I would judged it to be the darkest point of the nation's history. Such an act would only reveal the nation's arro-gance and its self-indulgence, as well as insensitivity and self-centeredness.

Defeating Japan should have been enough. Common sense tells us so (al-though what is common sense may be culturely different). Beating up the bully who had gone overboard in Asia should've been sufficient. Why, then, on top of it, did the United States have to insist on justice? What I, as a Japan-ese (although I don't claim to be a representative by any means), find hard to understand about the Tokyo War Tribunal is the way Americans turned blind eyes to all the wrongdoings their nation had done. I cannot help ask what sort of mentality it takes to do so.

If it were justice that had to prevail, you see, then the crimes committed by the United States against the Japanese had also to be examined. If it was retribution that was sought, the United States should have gotten it as the prerogative of the winner, but then justice should not have been brought in.

America wanted both justice and retribution, even though the two are mutually exclusive. This is the reason why the United States has resorted to self-deception and rationalization. Meanwhile many Japanese continue to entertain doubts about the Tokyo War Tribunal, trials where a criminal (Japan) was tried by a bigger criminal (the US). Clearly the United States should not have tried Japan, and clearly Japan ought to have protested. So, the question to ask is: how could such derailing on both sides occur?

THE NATIVE AMERICAN COMPLEX

Why then did America carry out such trials as the Tokyo War Tribunal? Why has she brought universal values such as civilization, peace and humanity — values no one can deny — to the table in trying enemies? Why did she deem violation of universal values a punishable offense? Why do many Americans believe they are the protector of universal values? The place to look for the answer, I believe, is their history.

Japan, you see, was not the first enemy Americans put on trial. At the end of the Civil War as you recall, the victorious Union tried the Confederates in a similar fashion. At their peace negotiation the Union demanded Confederates' unconditional surrender, rejecting the pleas presented by the latter, including keeping weapons. Only when the latter gave in and reluctantly agreed to surrender without any conditions did the victorious Union show a more magnanimous attitude. Seeing themselves and acting as the protector of justice — the one deciding who is good and who is bad — is an American way. And proclaiming being just is done after the enemy is cornered into unconditional surrender. Only when the enemy cannot object to any demands does America become lenient and forgiving. Such was certainly the case with the Japanese (although, as I have mentioned earlier, there were other factors operating there as well).

America, on the other hand, does not consent to be put on trial under any circumstances, or so it seems. During the Vietnam War, you might recall, North Vietnam suggested that air raids made by the US Air Force were against international law, a crime warranting a trial of the American pilots. Lyndon Johnson, then the President, was furious at this suggestion and countered the North Vietnamese with a threat that he might use atomic bombs against them. I remember this very well, as his anger seemed to be out of proportion. But here, I see a telltale sign of how American leaders see their nation's enemies.

There is a good reason, I think, why Americans want to keep justice on their side, and it stems from the history of having slaughtered the Native Americans. In order to build their own country on a continent already inhabited, the newcomers had to take the land away from the natives, but here, Americans (actually future Americans) were confronted by an insoluble dilemma. They had come to the New World to escape the corrupt systems of the old, you see, and they wanted to build a country where justice would prevail in the name of (their) God. Since such was their mission, they could not admit to the fact that they killed the natives they didn't want to be there. Some kind of self-justification was necessary. These newcomers must have believed that they were given the prerogative of absolute justice as the ones to fulfill a role given by their God; anyone who would block their way, therefore, had to be wicked, the ones who reject God's will. So believing, they formed a theory that anything and everything is permissible so far as those things eliminate the "bad guys."

Such was the idea around which Americans have shaped their identity. Were they not to insist that massacre of the native inhabitants was necessary and the right thing to do, therefore, the United States would have ceased to be the kind of nation they wanted it to be. Following the spirit on which the nation was founded, America without justice could not be America. To stop insisting that the massacre was necessary would mean the end of America. In order to avoid that happening, Americans need to keep convincing themselves that justice is on their side. This is how the United States has been rationalizing whenever it finds itself in a morally questionable situation. To put it more accurately, America has to perpetuate such situations compulsively so that it can go on rationalizing. It, in other words, has to somehow find a bad guy against whom it can fight, win, and impose punishment in the name of justice. This has to be done repeatedly, because otherwise its position as the promoter of justice will be weakened. Since self-rationalization is a form of self-deception, some amount of anxiety is inevitable. Thus, America has to perpetuate, just like a patient of compulsive neurosis does, the same conduct; it tries to convince itself that it is morally just.

If we look at US foreign policy as a chain of compulsive acts stemming from the original trauma of having murdered Native Americans, we might understand it better. Freud has written about a certain type of criminal whose sense of guilt makes him repeat the same crime. If I were to apply his psychoanalytic interpretation, the behavior of the United States is that of compulsive repeating. Just as it did in an attempt to annihilate Native Americans, America also has to go all the way in fighting without stopping or compromising in all other wars. It has to fight without trying to see the enemy's point of view, or, without an attempt to find a point where compromises can be made in order to stop the war. This is an American way.

Most Japanese don't find a resemblance, but it is not so far-fetched to imagine that many Americans identified the Japanese with their Native Americans; both of them, you see, are of the Mongol race. If the Japanese military leaders had studied US history and knew about the fate of the Native Americans, they might have had a better grasp of the US military. Instead, the Japanese held on to ridiculous notions, such as that American soldiers were a pleasure-seeking, jazz-and dance-loving bunch and that Japan might win the war if its brave and loyal soldiers fought with all their might.

In the Casablanca Conference of 1943, you may recall, President Roosevelt insisted on unconditional surrender of the axis. Churchill opposed this on the ground that it would unnecessarily increase casualties of the Allied Forces, but Roosevelt stubbornly held onto his position until Churchill conceded. I shall explain more of this below.

THE LOGIC OF DROPPING ATOMIC BOMBS

The way the United States government rationalized the dropping of atomic bombs is as follows: otherwise, US troops had to invade Japanese soil to force a surrender, and the battles would then result in as many as one million casualties (500,000 in another estimate) on the American side and ten times that on the Japanese. The bomb was necessary to save those lives.

There are logical flaws in this rationale. To start with, these figures had no basis. But even if the estimate for this theory was accurate, there is still a problem because the rational presupposed Japan's unconditional surrender as a necessity. The American rationale for dropping atomic bombs was based on this position of pursuing total surrender. The choice, in other words, was either dropping A-bombs or conducting land battles in order to beat Japan completely (so that she would accept any conditions). Given only those options, the dropping of the bombs was chosen, supposedly, reluctantly.

Japan, with disastrous news coming from various battlefields, knew by then that she had lost the war. She would have surrendered if a few conditions, particularly that of maintaining the imperial throne, were accepted. The United States, however, didn't want to accept anything but an unconditional surrender; conditions that might allow the people of Japan any amount of pride were unacceptable. A-bombs were necessary not to avoid large-scale casualties, but to force Japan to surrender unconditionally without retaining a trace of national pride. If America had not pursued this ultimate goal, I would say, the A-bombs were not necessary.

This, then, forces me to draw a conclusion that the United States resorted to A-bombs not as a better choice of the two disasters, but as a means to kill as many as possible. Dropping the bomb on Nagasaki in particular cannot be explained in any other way.

But why does America tend to persist in beating their enemy so utterly and completely? Because, psychologically, that's what they have done to their Native Americans. America cannot stop fighting until the enemy is completely knocked down because in the beginning they had beaten the Native Americans completely and they rationalized that act. They cannot allow themselves to see the enemy's points of view, nor to consider the possibility that some of the enemy conduct might be justifiable. If they did, they would be confronted with serious self-doubt: "Was it necessary to kill all those Indians, and why did we go that far?" It is too painful to try to answer this question. They have to prevent this self-doubt from surfacing. Thus, they must insist upon all enemies' unconditional surrender, and they have to prevent any other thoughts from emerging. What was justifiable in the past has to be just today as well in their psychic sphere. If what they do now were to be wrong, their past would have to be questioned. Then, their identity as Americans might collapse.

Let us now consider a more general situation. When a nation is in an antagonistic state with another, that nation has two options in fending off the antagonist. One is to either destroy the antagonist or keep it militarily weak and unmotivated for aggression (by infusing it with fear of retribution). The other is to make the enemy nation give up its hostile position by persuading it to turn around and become a friendly neighbor, or by impressing it with such high morality that the idea of attacking is unacceptable in itself. One does not have to cite the classic writings of Sun Tzu to see which of the two an ordinary (that is, healthy) nation would choose. The second choice is by far cheaper and without casualties; it is also more moral. This peaceful choice would also invite little criticism from a third party. Most nations would try this approach first, resorting to the other in a limited way and only when absolutely necessary.

It is my impression that the United States is a nation which opts for the first choice without much hesitation. Dropping A-bombs in fact was an extremely effective way to perform the task under this choice. The bomb infused such a great fear among the Japanese that they have entirely given up the idea of making the United States an enemy again. But this choice contains a certain danger. Suppose, for example, Japan were to have a nuclear capability and gain enough power to fight another war in the future; she then might use atomic bombs against America out of retribution, and the Japanese may feel they are free from an ethical or moral restriction in doing so. In other words, the choice of scare tactics has serious shortcomings. It requires constant guarding lest the enemy turn to retribution. Logically speaking, then, the United States used atomic bombs on the premise that there is no possibility of Japan's acquiring nuclear capability to go to war again, or, that such a development can be stopped. Nations which opt for the second choice would not have dropped atomic bombs. Considering the dangerous consequences, they wouldn't have placed themselves in the same situation as the United States was at the end of the Pacific War.

Among government and military leaders, as well as scientists who had helped develop them, were some who for various reasons were against using atomic bombs (Martin Harwit, *An Exhibition Denied: Lobbying the History of the Enola Gay*, 1996). There were also opinions that they should be aimed at combatants only and not at women and children; that the Japanese government should be warned beforehand as to where they would be dropped, that they should be dropped not on land but in the ocean, since the purpose was to show the bomb's power, etc. In the end, they were dropped without a forewarning and over a populated city, where there were no military bases or factories. Why?

Americans in general, it seems, do not consider the second choice mentioned above as a viable option—that of refraining from pushing the enemy into a corner, or stopping the war at a certain point so that the enemy does not develop a desire for retribution; establishing a long-term, friendly relationship to prevent future aggression is not their first choice. What they think of instead is either destroying enemies completely, or removing their capability to rebel. This, of course, was the strategy they used against their Native American.

In this type of thinking we see compulsive revisiting of the original act; it resembles the behavior of a neurotic patient who compulsively repeats the same unwanted behavior. This compulsive repeating, by the way, is not that of a mechanical kind, but is a pathological phenomenon of the mind where earlier unwanted behavior has to be repeated compulsively because of anxiety that stems from rationalization. And, rationalization cannot be easily thrown away because if it is, you end up with painful emotions (such as guilt), which you had pushed into the unconscious via rationalization. If the United States had chosen the second option in dealing with the entanglement with Japan, and if it were successful, Americans would have to face the inevitable question: why hadn't they done so with the Native Americans? It is a dangerous question with which most Americans are not prepared to be confronted.

AMERICA'S BLIND SPOT

I am inclined to say that the generosity shown in US occupational policies in Japan is related, as is the war-time cruelty, to the history of the massacre of the Native American, which has been rationalized as follows: we didn't want to annihilate them; we did our best to accept and live with them peacefully, putting their children in our schools and educating them so that they would become good citizens; it was not us who rejected them, for they insisted on keeping their barbaric ways instead of embracing our superior culture; and they closed the path for survival on their own, and there was nothing we could do but watch them destroy themselves; and so on.

Having killed many and cornered them into near despair in the war, the United States treated the Japanese in a fashion similar to that in which they had dealt with their native inhabitants. The Japanese, however, have made a fine recovery by taking American culture in enthusiastically; they have learned to create a nation of freedom and democracy. Considering Japan's post-war success in this light, Americans may have a superb alibi to rationalize their treatment of Native Americans. Look at the Japanese, they can say, here is a proof that we weren't wrong. It was the Native Americans who wronged themselves, because we have applied the same policies both times but one people was nearly annihilated, while the other is flourishing. Because they wouldn't give up their barbaric ways, Native Americans were punished, they can also say. We were only interested in doing what God's will called for, they even might add.

The more American culture the Japanese accepted (including its political philosophy), and the more like America Japan became, the more generous and supportive the US government became. It even bent backward to help. Realizing this, some Japanese (the Liberal Democratic Party, the Ministry of Industry, Trades and Information, the Ministry of Foreign Affairs among others) put a considerable effort into re-shaping Japan along lines Americans would want to see. As shown in rapid economic growth from the 1960s till the '80s, this strategy has been successful. The US government indeed has given Japanese industries a free leash so that they can export their products— televisions, tape recorders, motor bikes, semiconductors, etc. So much so that some of America's own industries were nearly destroyed. When Japanese technology was still undeveloped, Americans were not too particular about patents and industrial secrets. They were enormously generous.

Americans did not find out about the strategy taken by the Japanese government and industries at once, and the reason was, in part at least, because they didn't think too highly of the Japanese. They didn't think the Japanese could learn technologies and turn them into their own so easily. More importantly, however, Americans were under the spell of what I have explained as their "Native American complex." Their war-time attacks on Japan aiming at total destruction and defeat, their occupation, and Japan's rise to prosperity as the result of political, economical and educational reforms were all parts of the story Americans needed, so they could ease their minds of this complex. For the first time since their ancestors had founded their country, Americans had their dream fulfilled, the dream that they had failed in dealing with the Native American. And now, they were convinced, their culture had universal values acceptable to other races. One can say, therefore, that American generosity was not for the benefit of the Japanese; rather, it stemmed from a fear that their dream might be destroyed again, the fear existing more in the realm of the unconscious.

So, American generosity toward Japan in the post-war era was influenced by their historical guilt complex and their desire to be free from it. This is demonstrated in the kind of generosity shown in dealing with Japan, which hadn't been found in its approach toward Germany (although the United States was also lenient toward Germany, much more so than Britain and France had been at the end of World War One).

My interpretation of American involvement in Vietnam in view of their Native American complex is that Americans, having succeeded with the Japanese, went on seeking another chance to re-enact their dream, their story. Why else did US dispatch troops of no fewer than altogether 3 million soldiers to a small, far-away country in Asia, causing nearly 60,000 deaths and over 300,000 wounded, and losing 1,700 aircraft (fighter jets and bombers)? Why did it go on fighting as long as fifteen years until US economy began to suffer from war expenditures as high as 1.5 billion dollars? Why indeed when it neither coveted the land nor intended to exploit the people?

The standard answer to this question often-asked during the war was: because once Vietnam was taken over under a Communist regime, other neighboring countries would follow. This so-called "domino theory" shows that America's fear was neurotic in its nature. A person with dirt phobia, as we know, must wash their hands compulsively until they bleed, for fear that the dirt will spread to their entire body. America's approach to Vietnam is like that of a person with this phobia. The fear was unfounded, as Communist Vietnam did not affect other neighboring nations; the fear was that of anxiety neurosis.

According to psychoanalytic theory, neurotic anxiety is caused by repressing fear that has some basis in reality. The Vietnam war was fought because of America's repressed fear and because their dream was at stake. The Vietnamese might have been superimposed over Native Americans (as the Japanese had been) in the mind of ordinary Americans. If they were to accept the Vietnamese as they were, their logic went, then why hadn't they done so with the Native Americans? If they were unable to answer this question, their conscience would suffer; they would have to confront themselves with the notion that their treatment of the Native American had been wrong.

The Vietnamese therefore had to be conquered. Despite their insistence on maintaining their own culture, however, the Vietnamese were not defeated in the end. The severity of the shock Americans experienced at their defeat tells us how important it is for Americans to keep their dream intact.

Americans, however, were not deceived by the Japanese economic tactics for long. Some ("revisionists" they are called, and among them are James Fallows, Clyde Prescotts and Dutch journalist Karel von Wolforen) proposed that in view of economic conflicts with Japan, the United States should reexamine its view of Japan. They became aware of the Japanese strategy and began questioning the nature of the system behind it. They wrote that Japanese capitalism is of a different kind and that Japan is not a democratic nation. Many Japanese regard these revisionists as "Japan bashers." Some perhaps are, and they are merely trying to put Japan down. But there are other revisionists who are pointing out the fact that the US-Japan relationship has been based on America's wrong assumptions about Japan; they are proposing to draw a more accurate picture. By exchanging views with these revisionists, I believe the Japanese will be able to find a way to reach a perception of themselves more attuned to reality as well as mutually more satisfying.

What I also want to mention in relation to what I have explained above is the concept of justice. I think that America and Japan stand on opposite ends on this: one is a nation adamant about justice and the other is notably nonchalant about it. In Tokugawa Japan, for example, a standard decree on any type of argument was "guilty on both sides"; disregarding causes and rationales, people tended to believe that both parties were equally responsible. Japan still is a country where people try to reach a conclusion with the attitude of "if you all say so, let it be the way." Take the example of the Tokyo War Tribunal. People didn't object to (didn't seem to, at least) its outcomes, which in effect denounced them as criminals. (It is possible to see the acceptance of the outcomes as a case of Stockholm Syndrome). Most Japanese, I think, were totally unaware of malicious elements in the Tribunal's outcome and were merely puzzled why America acted the way it did. But, as I have said, Americans had a reason of their own.

Chapter Nine

Invasions and Apologies

As is the case with individual human beings, no nation can be all good or entirely bad. With no history of having invaded or colonized other nations, some are good, relatively speaking. There are others, like Mongolia, Spain, England, Portugal, France, Russia, Japan and the United States, with track records of invasion into other people's lands, with killing of many of the native inhabitants. But bad nations have good aspects, too, of course. There are nations that are both a victim and victimizer. China has been both the invader (of Tibet, for instance) and the invaded (by the British and the Japanese); so has Japan in its modern era.

We ought to see both the good and bad sides of countries clearly and with a sense of balance. We should be objective in assessing history. That Japan was threatened by the United States and that she invaded Asian nations, killing many people and acting arrogant, are both true. It is a fact that Japan's having fought against the Western powers gave other Asian nations the first step toward freeing themselves from colonizers. Japanese behavior, in other words, was neither all good nor entirely bad.

HYPOCRISY AND APOLOGY

A view that Japan, with her history of aggression, was entirely bad does exist. Seeing the country as the aggressive invader it once was, this view, taken by the United States in the Tokyo War Tribunal, can be referred to as the "Tokyo War Tribunal View of History," and lists reasons why Japan should feel guilty. It is not so difficult to understand why the United States took this view, but it is puzzling that some Japanese share the same position and regard the greater part of Japan's modern history as entirely bad. These people may believe that their position is the result of having faced-up and reflected upon all the things Japan has done, but to me their conclusion is one-sided. Just as it is wrong to turn blind eyes to the bad things Japan has done in order to draw a rosy picture, it is also a mistake to see the bad side only.

But what are the real motivations of these people who want to emphasize the bad side of their own country? Careful observation of them makes me realize that even though they are Japanese, they talk as if they are not, as if they are unrelated. They, in other words, point out and denounce various crimes Japan has perpetrated from the third party's point of view. In doing so they seem to think they are morally elevated. A misconception, of course, but blaming Japan is a proof for them that they are innocent. What's drawn in their minds is a sharp contrast between the pure and innocent self vs. a guilty and ugly nation—Japan.

Self-image of those who attack their country is that they are "clean and pure." They hope to disassociate, to be taken away as far as possible, and through bad-mouthing, they are crying out that they have nothing to do with Japan. You might call these people who seem to get satisfaction from listing their nation's faults and wrongdoing masochists, but I would rather define them as narcissists. Putting them in this light, we can explain many things about them. Imagine, for now, some African Americans who act as if they are not a part of their community, and imagine those who, having married a white and achieved social and economic success, despise other blacks who are poor and shabby. Those Japanese who point out only the negative aspects of their country are like these African Americans. They also remind me of people who are quick to denounce shortcomings of a group to which they once belonged. These people become critical at the first sign of outside persecution of their country, and they are more adamant than the outsiders, acting as if they had never been a part of it.

There are, of course, many Japanese who sincerely feel bad for what their country has done, and they believe Japan ought to show regret and apologize. They are genuinely sorry for the victims of Japan's aggression. They grieve for the crimes they did not commit themselves and feel responsible. What is the difference between these two kinds of people—those with genuine regrets and those who are interested primarily in their self-image as being clean and innocent? How do we distinguish one from the other? Although we humans are good at deceiving ourselves, looking at our subjective mind or how we feel does not necessarily help us here. Those who are motivated to promote a self-image may genuinely believe they are regretful, you see.

It is actually quite simple to distinguish the two. We need only to look at what they do, to see if their actions substantiate their opinions. If they, for example, use their own funds, or invest a great deal of their time and energy in helping the people of the countries victimized by Japan, those people are genuine when they say Japan ought to apologize. We must look at what actual help is being extended to the victimized and how many sacrifices are made willingly. No matter how eagerly and skillfully some well-known figures or social commentators argue for the necessity of Japan's apology (after all, they not only benefit monetarily by selling their pieces of writing, but also gain a reputation as being socially conscientious), or no matter how strongly they insist that Japan should compensate (not at their own personal expense), we should be skeptical unless their words are substantiated by actions.

There are reasons why we see a problematic, self-promoting insistence among some Japanese about Japan's apology. We may call those who ingenuously preach for apologies hypocrites, but the issue here is not as simple as leaving it at that. The problem, as I see, is with the Japanese as a whole rather than some individuals. For one, there is an issue of rationalization: to say, for instance, that haughty and stupid military leaders were responsible and that the public was simply deceived, forced, or put under a spell. By dismissing the past of their country as if it has nothing to do with Japan today, this rationalization neglects to examine the rise of militarism as an inseparable part of Japanese history. Or by denying a direct connection between the era before and after the war, people are deluding themselves. Hypocrisy and delusion, demonstrated by people who congratulate themselves that Japan's defeat has given the Japanese a chance for a fresh start, are merely a part of the large-scale delusions Japan has been suffering as a nation. It is a reason why those who insist on Japan's owing apologies find it hard to see their own delusion.

A WEAK LOGIC

This large-scale, national self-deception that transcends that of individual Japanese, a collective illusion, if you will, has been a dominant feature of Japanese society since the war. I was once labeled a rightist for using the term "Greater East Asian War," and this is an example of national self-deception (I don't necessarily insist on this term, but it seems a good one, as other names are less fitting: "Pacific War" won't do because then China is excluded, and "Asian and Pacific War" or "Far East War" sounds awkward). Easy labeling, by the way, was widely practiced during the war, when any criticisms or doubts about Japan's victory invited the name of "anti-Japanese." False illusions behind self-deception have shaky foundations, by and large, and as their structure is also weak, they easily collapse. Constant and nervous care are required, therefore, and a great deal of effort must be paid to suppress any objections or doubts. Although the directions are opposite, collective illusions in prewar Japan and those today are the same in nature. The practice of easy labeling in both cases is due to false collective illusions, and the intolerance toward the opposition, seen in both cases, reveals a weak foundation for both cases.

Speaking of apologies, the British have not apologized, even though they controlled India over several hundred years, exploiting people there and killing many of them. They have not apologized to China for their dirty Opium War, either. The French haven't offered an apology to the Vietnamese. Neither have the Dutch to the Indonesians. (Some years ago when Queen Beatrice visited Indonesia for the first time, she made a speech in which she unashamedly stated that, although the occupation benefited Holland, it also helped Indonesia.) The United States has not apologized for having dropped atomic bombs. Given these examples, some Japanese insist that no apologies are needed for the harm Imperial Japan has done to the people of neighboring countries. When Western nations don't apologize, they argue why should Japan?; after all, Japan committed atrocities only after the Westerners had done so, and on a much smaller scale. Some of these people also think the Japanese don't owe an apology because her advances in Asia were not invasions, at least not in an ordinary sense.

I recall a fellow student—an Englishman, at Strasbourg University, where I studied many years ago. This student, who knew a great deal about Japanese history—the annexation of Korea and what happened in Manchuria, etc.—hadn't heard about the Sepoi Rebellion. It made me wonder if English history education touched upon the Manchurian Incident, but not the Sepoi. I don't think that is the case now, but it is true that all nations tend to write their histories in such a way that they look good.

It is fine to be nationalistic, but one has to remain logically consistent, and those who are against Japan's apologizing disregard this consistency. Employing a logic that is clearly self-defeating, they speak their minds only as their mood dictates, it seems. It is as if they are merely saying that they don't want to bend first, or that they just don't like Western colonialism. I think they are merely saying what's convenient to them. If they insist that Japan owes no apology, they also have to say, to be logical, neither do Britain, France nor the United States. Arguing that Japan's control in Asia was to free Asians, while the Western powers were to exploit, has, as I have pointed out, a weak base to start with. Moreover, it brings Japan to the same level, for example, as the Dutch argument represented by their Queen.

I believe those who hold the position that Japan should apologize are also inconsistent. Among our politicians, for example, are those who openly proclaim that they hold this position. I suppose it is to oblige themselves to promote "for peace and friendship," which their constituency so adamantly insists upon. But they don't necessarily believe in such a position. They are merely giving lip service. Being without principle, they should be called political cowards. As I have said, consistency is what we need, and if an apology is called for, the reasons to do so should be very clear. Easy apologies, particularly via monetary compensations, invite troubles later on.

To be logically consistent, Japanese people should demand apologies where needed. If sexually exploiting women of an occupied land is a crime requiring an apology, as well as monetary compensation, the Japanese government should apologize and compensate those who were exploited in Korea and other nations. It should at the same time demand an apology and compensation from the US government for its occupational forces' having used Japanese women as "comfort women" as well. Whether or not the United States government would actually give any consideration to the matter is irrelevant. If the decision is to not ask for an apology for various reasons such as "it happened a long time ago" or "the United States is our ally now" or "it won't take the matter seriously anyway," then the Japanese should neither apologize nor compensate the Korean women. Regardless of which position is taken, we have to be logically consistent. Otherwise, the outcome will be that of having paid money and still being left with disdain.

THE EMPEROR'S RESPONSIBILITY

If Emperor Showa (Hirohito) is to be deemed guilty of war crimes, what would be the basis of that judgment? What is the logic behind it? In order to pass such a judgment we need two prerequisites: that the Greater East Asian War was a crime and that the sovereign or the head of state is responsible for that crime.

If the Greater East Asian War was a crime, against whom was it perpetrated? Among those involved in the war were, first, the people of East Asian nations who suffered during the war, then the Japanese, and lastly the Europeans and Americans. Out of these three groups, the Japanese don't qualify as victims because they were also victimizers. It is also questionable if the Western powers were the victims. The war between Japan and the United States, Britain and Holland can be seen as that between the two groups of aggressors and invaders victimizing the Asians. We cannot say, therefore, that one was the aggressor and the other was the victim. The usual formula doesn't apply here.

In order to try the Greater East Asian War as a crime, one must focus on the damage done to the people of East Asia. But the Tokyo War Tribunal de-emphasized this point and instead focused on the damage done to Western nations. But for now let's overlook this aspect and say that the Tribunal was to try Japan for having invaded other nations and exploited and killed their people. If what Japan has done is a crime, however, those committed by Western nations—Britain, France, Holland, the United States, Russia among others—are also crimes that require a trial. Having tried only Japan (and Germany) was inconsistent, indeed.

If the head of a state is to be responsible for that state's aggression, exploitation, and killing, furthermore, then British sovereigns, particularly Queen Victoria (who reigned during the Opium War), President Truman (who ordered the use of atomic bombs), and President Johnson (in escalating the Vietnam War) were all guilty of war crimes. If the responsibilities of these individuals along with the Emperor Showa were pursued, it would have been logical at least. The Tokyo War Tribunal is unacceptable to me precisely because the trial lacked this logical consistency.

There is an inconsistency in the manner in what the United States has behaved in the war tribunals. For instance, the one held in Manila ordered the hanging of General Yamashita Tomoyuki, the overall commander, for the cruelties committed by Japanese soldiers in the Philippines. He was made to take responsibility for what his subordinates (not directly below him, but those at the end in the line of command) had done. I recall that in an anti-Vietnam War rally in the States, some students were saying that if General Yamashita was guilty, so was President Johnson. To be logically consistent, the Tribunal should have made the Emperor Hirohito guilty as well, but it didn't. The occupational government must have seen the use of the emperor in governing post-war Japan. Logical inconsistency is found among the Japanese as well, however, since some among those who consider the Greater East Asian War an aggression are unwilling to pursue the emperor's responsibility.

In pursuing responsibilities for the war, not only those of the military leaders but of the Emperor Hirohito and the Japanese population in general should have been considered. That would be logically consistent. As I have mentioned earlier, the majority of the Japanese did not oppose the war. It is hard to imagine that when both the military and the public were inclined to think the war was inevitable, the emperor would oppose it. Some say that he was against the war but didn't have the power to stop it. This doesn't sound right, either. It must be a story made up afterwards. True, the majority of the military leaders were for the war, but if the emperor was staunchly against it, the war could have been avoided. If he had openly expressed his opposition, stating clearly that such a course would most likely destroy the nation, and must be avoided, there would have been no Greater East Asian War. The military couldn't have overruled the decision of the emperor, who was sacred, even if in words only. Remember the February 26th Incident (of 1936), which quickly ended, and the rebellious officers were severely punished? It ended in such a way against the military leaders' wishes, because the rebels angered the Emperor for having caused deaths of "His Majesty's faithful subjects." The emperor should have been able to make his will prevail this time too, since it was he who held the ultimate command, and the military couldn't have carried out its plan without his approval. If he had opposed the war and been insistent, some say, he would have been killed by an assassin's hand. This fear, according to the Emperor himself, was real. But still, questions remain.

My guess is that the Emperor himself saw the war as inevitable. It's no surprise if Hirohito wanted to emulate Emperor Meiji, his grandfather, who, having reigned in the era of the successful Sino-Japanese and Russo-Japanese wars, was enshrined in the Meiji Shrine. General Nogi Maresuke, who killed himself, following the demise of Emperor Meiji, was close to Hirohito, being one of his educators. Hirohito is a case similar to that in which a man repeatedly told the stories of his illustrious grandfather grows up wanting to emulate him.

Both the Emperor and the Japanese public were able to escape responsibility for the war. Only the military was made responsible. To push the entire burden to the party which no longer existed seems too easy a solution; a bit like bad-mouthing the dead when there is no fear of counterattacks. But then, most Germans and Austrians, too, seem to take the stance that the Nazis suddenly appeared from somewhere unknown, and that they themselves are not really responsible for what had been done under Nazism.

I am not necessarily for abolishing the emperor system. I believe that to separate authority from power and give the ruler authority without power is the best way of political governing. The most dangerous system is to give a dictator such as Hitler or Stalin both authority and power. The American Presidency also has both. (Since more recent presidents, like Nixon and Clinton, have behaved badly, damaging the authority of the presidency, we probably don't have to worry too much here.) There was a faction in Japan's pre-war era that strongly advocated giving both authority and power to the emperor, and this was the root of Japan's problems.

My position in supporting the emperor system is on the condition that the emperor has no power, at least to command the military. Having authority should be enough. If he has the final authority, those who have power are without authority. The public is less likely to accept power without authority. A situation such as that in Japan today, where people freely criticize the prime minister, is healthier. Although a yearning for a hero is hard to quench, a charismatic leader who is worshipped by the public is a real danger.

Chapter Ten

On Patriotism

Feeling cornered by the Western powers exerting pressures with their nationalistic ideology and practices, political leaders in Japan were resolved to shape their country after Western nations. In order to actualize this resolve, which was expressed in the slogan, "rich nation, strong military," they paid a great deal of attention to the task of infusing and encouraging patriotism. For over eighty years, from the fifth year of the new Meiji regime (1872), when the public educational system was established, until 1945, Japan's compulsory education focused, we might say, on making strong and patriotic soldiers out of the nation's students. We all know that this patriotic education has gone overboard, but the Japanese were under the spell of both fear of the Western powers and a competitive spirit.

Dying for one's country might be a noble deed, but throwing a life away according to the doctrine conjured up by foolish leaders (the military, its commanders and general staff) is another matter. It is particularly ludicrous when patriotism is coerced, and when one is not sure if it in fact is good for the country. The Japanese experienced too much of this patriotic coercion during the Pacific War, and in numerous examples they saw how miserable was the result of such coercion. Then, with the end of the war, came a reaction, and it took the Japanese to the other extreme. This shift was necessary, in part, to go along with the occupational government's policy.

In Japan, then, patriotism was a dirty word, a relic of their militaristic past, and anyone who made statements, such as "I love my country" was made a laughing stock as someone who was not altogether with it. Deaths of soldiers were now deemed useless. Post-war education under the strong influence of *Nikkyoso*, the National Teachers' Organization, tried to eliminate the spirit of patriotism from its educational agenda. Or so it seemed. Focus now was to be on individual rights. The new doctrine insisted that Japan had taken a wrong path because people, not seeing their individual rights as essential, had too readily sacrificed their lives for the country. Doing things for one's country was now considered foolish.

Japan today is split on the issue of patriotism and its symbols—the national anthem and the flag. As I see it, this split is a symptom of dissociation of the inner self from the outer self—one to promote and the other to oppose patriotism. To say which is right and which is wrong is, therefore, counterproductive. But I cannot say I understand the people who promote patriotism. Are they afraid that the public will forget about their country to the extent of allowing foreign invasions, that their nation will sink into oblivion? I have some doubts about people who propose to eliminate patriotism, too. Their argument makes me wonder if they think Japan otherwise will use aggression in the name of the good of the nation.

Patriotism, I think, is something like pride we have about our own country. Pride in us is a basis on which we build trust in ourselves, and it supports a sense that we are worth existing in this world, that our lives have a meaning. Having pride is important in this sense. So is patriotism, which I define as an illusion that one's own country is worthwhile. To put it in another way, an illusion that confirms the value of our individual life is somehow connected to the illusion that the country to which we belong has worth. If a person feels his life is worthless, that there is no meaning in it, he will inevitably lose a will to live, and die. Among the Japanese there may be some who think their country is without any worth, that it doesn't matter whether it exists or not. Japan would likely disappear if the majority subscribed to this view. If so, there's nothing one can do about it.

But I don't think there are many who agree with this view, that it doesn't matter if Japan disappears, wholeheartedly. At least I hope not. I don't want Japan to disintegrate. I want to believe that my country will be here after I die, that it will endure. Why? It's hard to answer this question, but perhaps because a part of my own ego is invested in the illusion called Japan.

The country in which we are born and raised is incorporated into our ego in various ways. I don't mean it is genetically predetermined, but our ego is shaped by many ideas, which are gradually shaped into a certain system. When we are born and raised as a Japanese or an American, the nation's past—its tradition, social consensus and common sense—are all going to be incorporated into our ego. That is to say various ingredients of the nation's past become materials to form our ego. Since they are incorporated into our individual ego, we cannot easily separate ourselves from our nation's history. One can either welcome or be repelled by these materials, but to dissociate ourselves from them entirely is not possible. There is no way to know how much patriotism an individual will pick up in the process of growing up, but little can be done about it.

As I have said, it is their instincts that tell animals how to live and act in the environment in which they find themselves, but we humans, with instincts no longer intact, need a different kind of guidepost, which is our ego. We select our behavior, relying on this guidepost, and we act based on what we are—a male or a female, a parent, a doctor, a student, a CEO, etc. If we are without ego, or the sense of self, we don't know how to conduct ourselves.

Our ego has to be supported by other people; without that support, it cannot exist. Unsupported ego is like the grandiose delusion of a mentally ill patient who believes he is Napoleon, for instance. Napoleon was Napoleon because the French public or people around him recognized him as such. We can say then that ego is a collective illusion born in our relationship with others. It, in other words, consists of a collective illusion supported by others.

A person (ego) and others who support that person form a group, and the first group we belong to is our family. We establish our place in the world as a son or a daughter born of a particular man and woman. This means that we human beings need family, not only to raise young children, but to establish our sense of self as well. Animals sever the ties with their children as they become self-sufficient, but humans retain the tie (identities of our parents and siblings). Otherwise our ego will not form itself into a good shape.

Just as an individual ego cannot be formed without others, families cannot exist by themselves, and they need to find themselves in the world around them. They need to belong to a larger entity such as a village or a community, and a community needs to belong to something larger as well. When people realize this seemingly endless chain of relationships, they begin to seek an existence that gives them a sense of finality, the ultimate being. And, they want this ultimate being to be absolute. Christianity, with its monotheistic absolute God, has served the function of the ultimate in Western culture. People supposed this only and absolute God created the world. Although they don't know how that God has come about, they stopped their thinking right there. As the belief in this God has weakened ("God is dead," someone has said, but not completely), modern nations emerged, perhaps to replace the old authority. For many people (not all, of course), this nation-state, with its absolutist ideology, became the basis for their ego. In a simplistic way of explaining, this is how nationalism was born.

Never having been monotheistic, the Japanese haven't experienced the process in a clear-cut way. What functioned as the absolute, I suppose, has been *ie* (family), which was to be inherited from ancestors and passed down to the future generation. It might have been a village with its shrine placed in a nearby grove, or, it might have been a local *han* (domains) and the shogun's government, which, by the way, was simply referred to as *okami* (up above).

The ultimate existence, the supporter of our ego, has to be eternal and supply absolute values. Since most of us cannot endure an awareness that our individual self is ephemeral, empty, and of little worth, we try to link ourselves to something sublime or absolute and eternal. Because we cannot locate such qualities within ourselves, we try to find them somewhere else.

This support of ego can be anything. If it is a group that gives the support, one's country may serve this purpose; it can be a religious group, or for segregationists, it may be a race-based group. The support can be abstract ideas rather than a concrete entity like a group or an organization. We don't have to get the support from only one source; we may get it from multiple sources simultaneously.

How, I often wonder, does the nation of Japan today serve as this support? I am sure some claim that their nation is not important and that they are unaffected by it. Others, on the other hand, are so devoted that they are willing to give their life for it. To keep in mind in considering either case is that it is natural for us to value and cherish whatever our ego is supported by. Because otherwise our *raison d'être* will be lost, our foundation shaken, and, possibly, our ego shattered. In order for a group to be able to provide the support needed by an individual ego, positive identification with that group via acceptance, affirmation, even affection, is necessary. It is this identification that affirms our ego. Thus, not believing in the value of the group to which we belong is not to believe in our worth as an individual. How much support does a person born and raised in Japan or America receives from being Japanese or American is determined by various factors, but unless there are some extenuating circumstances, a certain amount of support is naturally there.

To cherish, to respect, and to love one's country is what we call being patriotic. Then, we can determine how patriotic a person is by seeing how much ego support he(she) derives from his(her) country. Those who find their country is providing no support naturally have little or no patriotism, and it is useless to force them to be patriotic. If, on the other hand, their country occupies an important place in their ego's support system, those people are naturally patriotic, and it is no use for others to criticize or try to exert influence on them to be otherwise.

If patriotism is lacking among the Japanese today, it is not because it hasn't been taught but because it was taught as something negative. If we don't teach it as bad, patriotism will grow naturally, more or less, without anyone working hard at it. We naturally have positive feelings toward the country we live in; most of us like the place where we were born and raised, where we have some fond memories. To me, this emotion that naturally flows out of us is enough. There is no need to use such a big word as patriotism. The important point is not to deny that such an emotion does exist and realize that there is nothing one can do if it doesn't. Education with the aim of promoting patriotism or eradicating it are both an attempt at meddling.

Patriotism that is not the outflow of a genuine emotion has no place, and extreme and blind patriotism is problematic, to say the least. If Japan's Ministry of Education were to further extend its ambition, it might encourage such a kind of patriotism; it might push patriotic education with both *Kimigayo* and *Hinomaru* (national anthem and flag), both of which are now formally recognized as the nation's legitimate symbols. It is the habit of the bureaucrats to pursue, single-mindedly and excessively, whatever they set as a policy. If the task is set to promote patriotism as a part of the nation's educational goal, they will not practice moderation. They will go to the extreme, and the reaction to that will be further confusion. Suppose the Ministry insists on a kind of patriotism that emphasizes Japan's greatness and splendid features and presses teachers with such a guideline, and suppose teachers feed it to their students mechanically; would that accomplish patriotism? Quite doubtful. Since patriotism is a matter of heart, it can be transmitted to students only by teachers who hold it in their hearts; it is not the area in which the Ministry of Education has any role whatsoever.

As I have said earlier, my position is that instincts of our human species have been "broken down." We usually associate instinct with something like "blind urge to do anything one pleases," but this is a definition of "brokendown" instincts. Animals' instincts, which are intact, can inform them, for example, not to fight with others unnecessarily, not to invade others' territories without reasons, not to violate the rules of the herd, and not to mate other than at a fixed time and in a certain manner; some animals even follow rules which are similar to what we call laws and morality. They wouldn't be able to survive in their natural environments otherwise. Their instincts, in other words, function not only as an accelerator but also as a brake, and when I say human's instincts are broken down, I mean this brake is not functioning. Both laws and morality of the human species are not so reliable because they are man-made, but we still need them; we have no choice but to create them artificially. Thus education, through which laws and morality are pounded in.

Undoubtedly, laws and morality have to be pounded into our children through education, but we have some difficult questions to ask: what kind of laws and morality do we teach and who does the teaching? Those in charge of shaping educational policies usually belong to a circle who rule the country, and they tend to go for force feeding what's convenient to them, disregarding the needs of children themselves. We all know how disastrous is the outcome of such an approach. The opposite to this, the laissez-faire approach of believing in children's "unlimited potential" and of letting them "grow up freely," however, will turn our children into monsters; they will grow up to be either reckless and uncontrollable or selfish and self-centered. We are seeing the result of such an approach rather clearly today.

The issue is not as simple as choosing a laissez-faire approach or authoritarian indoctrination. If we choose the latter, we will end up with men and women looking more like mechanical dolls with no spirit, but choosing the former means we will have monster-like individuals. Defending the laissez-faire approach because of the problem of authoritarianism, or rationalizing the authoritarian approach because of the shortcomings of laissez-faire are both gravely mistaken ideas. The inherent problem, I think, is to try to link education to a doctrine of one kind or another.

It is not terribly surprising, and it is not the end of the world, if there are some Japanese who dislike Japan. To say something like "if you are Japanese, you ought to love Japan, otherwise you should leave" is to take the matter to an extreme. However, if we are to compare two kinds of countries—one with a majority of people not liking their country and not caring what will happen to it, and the other with people who cherish their country as a good place worth defending against any dangers and threats, it is clear that the former receives less esteem internationally, which in turn brings disadvantages to its people. It is the same with an individual person. Those who have low self-esteem tend to be less appreciated, if not ignored. But, if there are people who worry that the Japanese are not patriotic enough, I'd say to them: there is nothing we can do but to wait for that sentiment to grow naturally. It is not a concern of the Ministry of Education, which has no authority over it nor the capability to properly deal with it.

In its overzealous attempt to create a nation capable of countering Western powers, the Japanese government had tried to implant patriotism in the public in a hurry via the Ministry of Education. After the war, as a reaction, the National Teachers Union decreed patriotism the cause of all evils. Today, the Ministry does not openly endorse patriotism and the Teachers Union exerts much less influence. Yet it is my position that any organizations holding a fixed idea about educational policies, be it the Ministry of Education or Teachers' Union, should be eliminated entirely. I have been a long-time advocate of eliminating the Ministry of Education, but the Teachers Union is also a harmful organization under which to educate the nation's children. My proposal, therefore, is to follow the dictum of "it takes two to tangle," and get rid of them both.

It is wrong to decide what is "the right approach" to education and apply it throughout the country, whether it is done through the Ministry's guideline or as the result of votes at the annual assembly of the Teachers Union. My idea of good education is to allow individual teachers to teach according to their own ideas. They should be allowed to do so as long as they will not force other teachers to follow, will not attack those who disagree, and will not organize groups in order to disseminate their ideas. There will be differences in individual teacher's approaches, but biases and extremes will work against each other, finding eventually a neutral and decent point to settle. Ideas can be anything—patriotism, communism, emperor worship, liberalism, pacifism, laissez-faireism, militarism, individualism, democracy, authoritarianism, or no position, for that matter. What has to be avoided is to pick one idea and propose that everyone adopt it, deeming it the right idea. Principles and ideologies are, to me, all illusions; they are all one-sided and prone to be self-congratulatory. One ought to be able to believe in the idea of one's own choice. History has shown us that insisting on one position as the right one brings nothing but disaster. To attempt unity in education by forcing either authoritarianism or the laissez-faire approach is wrong.

Afterwords

Would it be possible for America to see her history in a more balanced way by analyzing her own behavior in successive incidents that involved Japan? This was the question I had in mind in writing this book. By analyzing incidents such as Commodore Perry's threat, anti-Japanese immigration polices, the Hull Note, the massive air raids on the Japanese lands, the atomic bombs, occupation, and the Tokyo War Tribunal? Would it be possible for her to look into her own hidden motivations and reasons beyond those which people have believed to be rational? Would this be helpful in understanding hidden motivations in the American psyche that seems to have driven her in more recent wars? And where people see they were wrong, could they apologize? In case of the Japanese, I believe they would be satisfied with an apology, if it is only for having dropped atomic bombs, and an apology would make Japan surrender her rationale for ever using nuclear weapons even if Japan were to ever possess them in the future. Then America's major fear about Japan, which I presume has been repressed into the unconscious realm of its collective mind, would be dispersed.

If Americans were to bring their complex about Native Americans into full consciousness and analyze it carefully, perhaps they could overcome it, and that might result in their apology, for instance, to the Japanese. The course of action taken in so-called "fighting terrorism" may then change. Until that happens, Americans will continue to see the ghosts of Native Americans in the Japanese and other people; they will remain overly sensitive; they will repeat inaccurate observations and demonstrate misguided behavior. Similarly, if the Japanese were to overcome their internal split of the outer and the inner self and apologize, then the two nations would be able to have a truly meaningful and friendly relationship. Until that happens, the Japanese will continue to hold grudges against the United States in their inner selves, while acting otherwise, smiling humbly and letting America continue to dominate. If the important task is to establish a truly cooperative relationship, then, the most important thing is not to talk about what to sell and what to buy, but to look at the fundamental structure of the relationship itself.

The method to be used to overcome the Native American complex is the same as that used in treating neurosis caused by early childhood trauma. It can be done by deciding not to hide, or warp, the facts about the nation's past and the way it has dealt with Native Americans; it can be done by stopping to rationalize and face the facts squarely. It is possible by understanding how the nation's past is related to its behavior today.

Appendix

Psychoanalysis Applied to Groups and US-Japanese Relations

In this book I treated countries, the United States and Japan, as if they were individual people. I discussed and analyzed actions taken by these countries, or behaviors demonstrated by their people, as if they belong to individuals, applying psychoanalytic theory. I touched upon reasons why this equation is valid in the text, but I want to summarize and highlight them here as well.

I believe we human beings are animals whose instincts are broken into pieces: Broken, but not lost. Broken and now in pieces, they nonetheless exist, but they don't function as guidelines for our actions and behaviors. Animals use their instincts to recognize their natural environments, deciding how to act in response to the reality of their particular environment. We humans, however, cannot recognize our reality as a unified entity because it is shattered, as it were. We have lost the reality to which we are to adjust in a coherent manner. Unable to see what surround us clearly, we don't know how to conduct ourselves.

Having lost sight of our reality, we have allowed some gaps to be created, and in the schism of these gaps floats our energy, unfocused and separated from reality. And this energy, according to my theory, hitches itself to various illusions coming in from outside. These illusions do not accurately reflect our reality. In individuals, they stem from shattered self-recognition, and if they are handed down from other people, they are merely a consensus, often without a realistic basis also. We call both types of these illusions the human psyche. Animals do not suffer from gaps between themselves and the realities of their natural environments. Since there is no schism, there is no psyche.

We humans are under the control of various unorganized illusions, which must be assembled into some kind of structure to function as behavioral guidelines. Our ego is shaped by these structured illusions, and it sits at the center of our psyche. In place of instincts it is primarily this ego that dictates our action. This ego, a body of illusions, if you will, is organized according to certain standards and norms. The part that does not fit them has to be eliminated. That is, not all illusions that harbor in our psyche can enter our ego. Those eliminated are, in fact, far more numerous. Although we can be conscious of only those illusions that have become a part of our ego, those eliminated, that is, illusions that remain in our unconscious mind, also influence our behavior one way or other. Although we choose our actions or make decisions according to how we define ourselves—as a man, woman, parent, child, the company president, or as a Japanese, a student, etc.—usually, on rare occasions we lose our control and let our impulses dictate. Sometimes we also rationalize, unconsciously or subconsciously.

Unlike natural instincts, our ego has no basis in hard reality (such as biological functions and natural environments); it, therefore, has to be supported by various illusory devises. Time, for instance, is a human invention; it is one of ego's supporters, or to put it in another way, time houses ego. Ego can exist and find its place so far as it is in something like time. In other words, there is no entity called ego. Our ego is mere locality.

Since it exists in time, ego has to have a beginning, an origin. The idea of a father and a mother is useful, and they, too, have to have their own father and mother. It is in this way that ego finds its connection to a group as well as to the past. It, in other words, has a story that began sometime in the past, goes through the present, and will be passed on into the future. One might say that ego is the story of ego itself. A stone can undeniably exist without any explanations, but ego cannot exist without its story. To say that ego finds itself in time, that it has a story of its own, therefore, means it has a beginning and an end. We thus fear death, a feature unique to humans.

Our ego needs to be framed by values as well. Animals are not bothered by such questions as identity, purpose, and the meaning of life. Not being firmly grounded in realities, supported by ego entrapped by the framework of time, humans cannot live without a sense of value and of uniqueness (ego identity). We have to be able to believe that we are connected to something long lasting, even eternal. So that we can escape a sense of emptiness, uncertainty, and uselessness (or death). That's why we entertain various ideas with eternal value: God, country, family, justice, truth, beauty, art, revolution, race, and so on.

As I have said, human behaviors are determined by our psyche, a certain structure formed artificially in the gaps where instincts were once, and this structure is constructed with various illusions. Rather than instincts and biological factors, then, our behaviors have to be explained by the kinds of illusions we have and how those illusions are being formed into various aspects of our culture.

Freud examined the structure of human psyche in terms of its three parts—super-ego, ego and id. As you know, super-ego is made up with norms and morality (the part geared toward ideals is sometimes specified as "ideal ego"); ego is an organization in charge of adaptation to reality, and id is the impulse that goes against morality (super-ego) and ego (reality). Although these three facets can function in unison, most of the time they don't. Super-ego and id are usually against ego, or, super-ego may join ego and stands against id. Or, ego and id may join their forces against super-ego. The three elements, in other words, find themselves in various shapes of conflict, and if conflicts are not resolved reasonably well, certain outcomes or endeavors unique to human beings, such as neurosis, crime, art and other activities, will result.

Shifting our attention away from individual human beings, let's now look at groups. Groups we humans form, such as tribes and nations, do not rely on instincts like those of ants and bees. We create groups based upon our illusions. Just as a multitude of our individual illusions are structured into our psyche, the schism created between the groups and their natural environments is formed into a humanistic world (culture). Having lost an ability to accurately see and adjust to the reality of our natural environments, in other words, we have created our psyche internally, and a humanistic world outside of us. We have tried to fill the gaps between ourselves and shattered realities by letting our psyche live in the humanistic world we created. Such an endeavor was necessary for our survival, but needless to say, the gaps have never been completely filled.

Although a multitude of illusions we human have are structured in such a way that they can become a part of our psyche (at the center of which is our ego), various problems can arise in the process of this structuring. For instance, if ego pays too rigid an attention to certain illusions while repressing others that are contradictory, the psyche finds itself in an extremely difficult situation. Ego may fluctuate between the two conflicting illusions, causing the psyche to split, or, it may be immature and weak because structuring hasn't gone well. While ego has to accommodate various inclinations of unorganized and scattered illusions (it is not possible to accommodate all the illusions, many of which are mutually contradictory to start with, but excessive denial would lead to the collapse of psychic structure), it at the same time has to adjust to, and live in, both the natural and cultural environments. The two tasks are contradictory by nature.

Now our world, shaped with natural environments as ingredients, must be the kind of place where our psyche, or structured illusions, can live both safely and sufficiently close to reality. These two demands are also contradictory. To simplify, too much emphasis on the well-being of our illusions will cause maladjustment to the reality we live in, but if emphasis is on the adjustment to the reality, ignored illusions will cause psychic discontent.

Our inner psyche and our outer world are both man-made; they are cultural products. While our psyche is made up of pieces of broken instincts, the world is shaped by broken, sometimes lost, pieces of realities. Both are the product of unorganized illusions. Since our psyche is molded in such a way that it can exist in the world, and the world is shaped to accommodate our psyche, the two correspond to each other. Both, in other words, have the same structure.

The problem, however, is that just as our psyche is not exactly the same as the broken instincts that have formed it, the world is not exactly like an original broken and lost reality. Although the gap in both cases is inevitable to an extent, if it is too large, it will destroy us. If the gap between our psyche and original instincts is huge, mental illnesses, such as paranoia and grandiose illusions, will result; too large a gap between the world we live in and the original reality will prevent us from adjusting to that world and accepting the reality. For the Japanese who lived in the world of the "Great Empire of Japan," for example, adjusting to that world could mean their real lives were to be destroyed.

Just as our individual psyche has to have a certain structure, groups, such as tribes and countries, have to shape various illusions entertained by their members into a coherent unity. As with an individual, a group or a nation has to adjust to its outside world while maintaining various illusions, so that members are kept sufficiently happy. It needs a structure similar to that of Super-ego, ego and id, and that structure may consist of three elements of the emperor, the government and the public. (The emperor represents authority, norm, and morality, while the government takes care of administering them; the public can be motivated by, or function according to, desires and impulses.) Freud explained how repressed impulses find ways to express themselves in various round-about ways (symptoms) in an analogy of a government suppressing unwanted public opinions (suppression results in diverse modes of expressions such as irony, satire and other literary work). This is more than analogy. Stemming from a structure with similar weaknesses, the two can be considered as the same phenomena.

Realities in which human groups exist are without solid foundation (such as biological functions, natural environments, etc.), and they have to be supported by various kinds of illusion. This is why groups, as individuals, have to exist in time; they have to have histories. There are no tribes and nations without a myth about their origin. The Japanese, for example, had a myth that gods had created their race/tribe. Just as an individual may suffer from some neurotic symptoms because of a now-forgotten trauma, painful incidents of a long-gone era, about which no official documentation may be available, sometimes affect the members of a tribe or a nation, influencing their behaviors.

In his article "The Man Moses and Monotheism," Freud interpreted *the Exodus* drawing upon a description of a neurotic patient who has repressed his memory of early childhood. Repressed memories, he says, are the memories that have been falsified, those that come about through suppressing, or hiding, traumatic incidents. Facts that make us feel uncomfortable may be falsified, or something that didn't actually happen may be added. Re-reading of these false memories gives us a clue in understanding the causes of neurosis. Moses supposedly led the people of Judea to escape Egypt around the 14th century BC, but Freud has a different version. Moses was not Jew, he says, and furthermore, there were two Moses, one of whom was killed by the Jews. These facts had been denied, says Freud, and it is this denial that became a backdrop for various elements of Judaism, such as Messianic beliefs and the idea of a contract with God, as well as the branching off of Christianity and its concept of original sin. In other words, incidents of the fourteenth century BC, afterwards repressed, formed Judaism and Christianity as we know them today.

Freud also explained how our memories of early childhood affect us and help form various neurotic symptoms in terms of unconscious memories. Although erased in our conscious mind, that is, early childhood memories remain in our unconscious minds and influence our behavior. If we are to explain the case of individuals this way, we should also be able to say that memories of a group that were forgotten for several hundreds or thousands years affect how things are with that group today. For individuals, we could say that old memories were left somewhere in our brain cells, but what about with groups? Where is the site of those ancient memories, and how are they transmitted to the descendant?

The only way to answer this question, it seems, is to hypothesize an entity, something like a collective unconsciousness, where memories are stored to be passed down to posterity as if it's the work of genes. I find it difficult to accept this hypothesis, and if the hypothesis is difficult to apply to groups, so is to the case of individual people. Because individual memories and those of a group are similar phenomena, both have to be explained by the same hypothesis.

What we misunderstand, I believe, is the nature of human memory. Memories are not like pictures taken by a camera or footprints made on sand, a trace we leave behind. They are nothing like mechanical entities. But, because we tend to understand them as something that has physical characteristics, we end up understanding them to be traceable, or, as something mysterious like collective consciousness.

If, on the other hand, we define memories as conjectures we make about our past using materials available to us, we will be able to solve the dilemma mentioned above. Memories, in other words, are not enduring pictures nor resurrections of the past, but rather, they are something we reconstruct constantly. In our memories of early childhood scenes, for example, we sometime see ourselves in those scenes. Since seeing us there is not possible, those must be our memories with newer elements added as we imagine them.

By understanding them as "the best conjectures we can come up with based on materials that are available to us," both collective memories and individual memories can be explained under one consistent hypothesis. Histories of races or nations tend to be rewritten when an empire has fallen under a new ruler, or when a revolution has taken place. And they are rewritten in a way most convenient to the current regime. It is the same with an individual's history and memories. When our ego is reconstructed, our forgotten memories are revived and our past is reshaped accordingly. For example, when a son who's been dependent on his mother acquires independence, the image of a gentle and dedicated mother may subside, and now he can remember his mother as having been cold and self-centered. The case may be the other way around, and the man becomes more independent because the old image of a cold and self-centered mother has come back. Similarly, it is often not clear whether revolution happens because of a tyrannical regime, or the revolution makes the old regime appear tyrannical.

The same can be said about distinguishing genuine memories from false memories. By considering memories spatially, thus seeing unwanted memories placed in a sphere called the unconscious (repression) while letting convenient but false memories take over in our consciousness, we are saying that one entity, genuine memories, and the other, false memories, are located separately. Instead, we might consider as follows: genuine memories are the logical conclusions we reach by letting our materials in hand take a natural course of conjecture. False memories, then, are something that were forced upon us. Genuine memories are those that come back, despite strong repression or denial, because they are the inevitable result of our thought processes and not because they are powerful.

"Materials in hand" should be taken in a broad sense as something more than our conscious mind can recognize. When we try to understand our early relationship to our parents, for example, we don't rely exclusively on what we can remember about them—their behaviors, actions and words. Experiences of parental violence or abuse, which affect our personality, the way we think and feel, and the way we relate to our friends and lovers are also important materials. Our past leaves its traces clearly on our present, and all those traces from remembering and reconstructing our past are also our materials.

A nation's past history is marked not only in its official records and documents, but also in legends, folklore, fairly tales, crime stories, literary works, plays and songs as well as in festivals, rituals and various customs. There is no past that doesn't affect the present, and in this sense the past can never be lost. Even when a certain political regime tries to deny its tarnished past, pretending it never existed, the effort of denial itself makes that unwelcome fact rise to the surface. It is like the sign that says "Don't throw trash here."

Now, let's go back to the case of individuals once again. Even in our adult life, we make new and spontaneous judgments on our parents, perhaps unconsciously, and on those occasions we use a large body of materials our past relationship with them has left with us. These unconscious judgments are often more to the point than conscious ones; they are more encompassing. Take a situation frequently presented by clinical psychoanalysts, like that described in Freud's "Notes on a Case of an Obsessive Neurosis." Perhaps the patient in this case loves and respects his father very much in his conscious mind and is willing to sacrifice himself, but unconsciously, he hates him and wants to kill him. I propose to understand this case as follows: although the patient has judged unconsciously, based upon a large body of materials in hand, that his father deserves his hatred, some immediate reasons or realistic circumstances have persuaded him to believe that he loves him, or he in fact does love him, to a degree. A conflict in this love-hate relationship, that of a positive assessment of the father and a negative judgment of him, is based on the result of accumulated materials from many years back. In other words, it is not between the love located in the conscious and the hate found in a sphere called the unconscious.

Conflicts commonly seen in our relationship with our parents are similar to those found between two nations, the United States and Japan, for example. The Japanese view of America in the modern era has been split into two extremes, and as I described in this book, it fluctuates between pro-American sentiments and anti-American feelings. The structure we see here seems to be similar to that of Freud's neurotic patient, who consciously loves her father but also hates him on the unconscious level. But we don't have to rely on such an ambiguous hypothesis as the memory of the collective unconscious to draw a connection between the Perry incident and the Japanese attitude toward the US-Japan relationship today. There are innumerable marks stamped on the US-Japan relationship of a hundred and some years, and on those vestiges stands the current US-Japan relationship. One cannot say that the incident has nothing to do with Japanese people today simply because Commodore Perry's arrival in Japan was long ago and no Japanese who lived then are here now.

Innumerable illusions that shape a group (Japan, for example) and those that make up individuals (the Japanese) are the same, more or less. If you were born and raised in Japan, and if your psyche was shaped accordingly, illusions that have come into your psyche are those held by the group of people around you. Even if you are to create your own illusions, you cannot escape from being influenced by those held by the group of which you are a member. Which parts of group illusions one incorporates, however, differs from person to person, and even if a same illusion is taken in, it is up to the individual to decide where to place it; which illusion to place at the center of one's ego and which to push down into the realm of the unconscious is one's choice.

Simplifying the matter, let's for now suppose there are two kinds of illusions among the Japanese—pro-American and anti-American. The Japanese government in the pre-war era held polices of anti-USA and suppressed (repressed) pro-American illusions. After the war, it picked up the pro-American position, rejecting illusions of anti-Americanism. Similarly with individual people, some have chosen to place pro-American illusions at the core of their ego, while others have done so with anti-American illusions. In the former case, anti-American illusions were there, although repressed, and the latter, the other way around. So far as the entire content of illusions is concerned, both are more or less the same.

Psychic patterns of an individual and a structure of a group are quite similar in basic shapes and contents, and that is why I proposed in this book to discuss historical and current issues of the US-Japan relationship, applying one method to analyze both of them. I am not merely forcing psychoanalytic theories of the individual into group situations. To me, psychoanalysis is fundamentally a study of group psychology.